"This book is chock full of powerful information that should be read by *anyone* planning to start *any* business."

J. Morris *retired small business banker*

Praise For The Writings Of
David Evert

"I wish all my clients had read your books before meeting with me. They would be so much more organized." *Ross, Restaurant Designer*

"Thank you for writing your books, you are now my coffee business GURU." *Mimi, Espresso Express, Florida*

"Your books are a great help, even here in Mexico." *Susan, Amigos Coffee, Mexico*

"I am so glad to have your books. My son and I are now working on the same mission, creating a consistent feel in the business and that makes all the difference." *Joanne, Brewed Awakenings, MN*

"I don't think we could have gotten this business started without your help. The books were so helpful and encouraging." *Patty, Royal Cup, MN*

"David, you and your books saved me at least six months and so many thousands of dollars getting my business started. I am so pleased."
Kris, Caffe LeGrande, MN

"You're not a literary genius, but those books you write carry a powerful practical and pragmatic punch." *Ron, Java Trout, WI*

"Your books made this entire project easier to organize. I never felt overwhelmed. We saved at least six to nine months time and many thousands of dollars and I know I am enjoying the business more because of what I learned from you." *Peggy, Coffee Depot, IA*

"I do not know that we six owners could ever have gotten this business started without your books. You gave us the encouragement we needed and a simple method of preceding that resulted in a single business out of six creative minds. Thank you for your books and your consulting help." *Connie, Aromas, MN*

"If you want a winning game plan, listen to your coffee coach. David Evert's new book covers all the right fundamentals in building a successful retail coffee business." *Ted R. Lingle, Executive Director SCAA*

"Another great tool designed to take the guesswork out of opening a specialty coffee business. Buy it!" *Ward Barbee, Publisher, Fresh Cup Magazine*

THE Coffee Coach

David Evert

How To Start A Successful Coffee and Espresso Business

The Play-by-Play Guide

This publication has been sponsored by
and is distributed under the direction of
The Coffee Academy™, *a division of*
Espresso Midwest™, *Minneapolis, Minnesota.*

The Table of Contents

Thank you, Thank you, Thank you.

A Personal Greeting From the Author

Introduction

Section I *What Is Required To Be An Entrepreneur?*

Section II *The Coffee Opportunity*

Section III *Plan Your Work*

Section IV *Work Your Plan*

Section V *Rounding Up The Little Things*

Appendixes

There are so many people to thank!

The content of this book is an orderly presentation of the highlights we have learned over 30 years during which time countless individuals have shared ideas, knowledge and instruction that I now share with you.

For sure, there are hundreds of suppliers, customers, roasters, friends and competitors who deserve appreciation for their gifts to my experience.

There are some specific individuals who cannot go unmentioned. Pat Kadlec and Denise Llanas have been my patient and understanding partners for all these years. Thank you for your support, tolerance and encouragement.

Allen Plante provided the persistent prodding I needed to undertake and finish this project. Jeff Bell of *Drugstore ZEN Press* helped me do what I could not accomplish on my own, consolidate the three previous books into one single coherent book. Amy Barron, whose professional and objective critique has added so much of the little detail, produced some of the largest impact.

I want to especially thank Jim Morris, Dick Oberle and Carol Spearman whose persistent encouragement and criticism have strengthened the metal of my character and the strength of my convictions.

I also want to thank all of those whom I may never meet, editors, lay out specialists, graphic artists, printers, web masters and on and on.

For all of those I wish to thank, let it be known that this publication is truly the fruit of their work to which I humbly sign my name as author.

Certainly, all past and present employees of Espresso Midwest have been a great inspiration to me.

Kent Bakke, Joe Monaghan and Pat Lorass of Espresso Specialists: Thank you for the knowledge and guidance that led me into this business and the professional role modeling that I have aspired to copy these many years.

I dedicate this book to each and every aspiring entrepreneur with this quote from Beverly Sills, *"You may be disappointed if you fail, but you are doomed if you don't try."*

A personal greeting from the author.

The purpose of this book is to help people who are considering a coffee business of their own to confidently move forward. Some of you will learn from this book that coffee is not what you want to do, but you will learn many valuable lessons that apply to any other business you might choose. Many of you will be encouraged by this book and will successfully apply the knowledge and tools we provide to become new coffee business owners. Whichever path you choose our purpose will have been achieved.

It seems that a great place to start, is to give you some history on the author that will provide you confidence this book will indeed be valuable to you. I have enjoyed helping others succeed in this specialty coffee market for more than ten years. The content of this book takes you through all the steps clients go through in a personal two thousand dollar face-to-face consulting project but you get to do so at a fraction of that cost and at your own pace.

I became aware of the exciting world of specialty coffee in April 1988. It so entranced me that I moved to Seattle immediately where I could continue my corporate job and also investigate and research the coffee business first hand. My best friend Pat and I decided to launch a retail business in Minneapolis and brought in Denise as the third partner in the fall of 1989. That company, Caffe` Amore` was ultimately grown into a seven-site chain before we sold it to folks who blended it into a larger regional franchise roaster/retailer company.

Before the end of our first year in business as Caffe` Amore`, we had become quite disappointed with the lack of help from our suppliers of espresso equipment, carts and coffee. They all seemed to know their own business, but while they had many opinions, they really showed no interest, personal understanding or knowledge to help us successfully operate and grow our retail business.

We felt like many suppliers were only interested in us until our check cleared and after that we were left to go it on our own. We were frustrated and felt taken advantage of, misled and abandoned. We already could see, in 1990, many mistakes we could help others avoid. The success we did achieve in that retail business could have been so much more and so much easier with the right kind of advice and help. We decided to provide that help.

While my partners grew Caffe` Amore` into a successful chain of retail outlets, I proceeded to do in-depth organized research and study to create a set of "how to" manuals to help people enter this business better prepared than we had been.

The resulting manuals were published in late 1992, and because of the demand for this type of help in the Midwest, I moved back to Minneapolis where we started a company to distribute the books, offer new business consulting, supply specialty coffee equipment, and provide training and service for coffee and espresso machines.

The content of the books was organized into a one-day seminar in 1996. That class, which continues to be highly popular, has now been shared with over 700 people. The books were updated in 1997 to give readers the benefit of more lessons learned and more current industry information.

If all you learn from this reading is how to avoid mistakes others and we have made ahead of you, it will prove to be one of your most valuable investments

Starting in 1993, through 2002, I have coached and mentored more than 600 people through the process of opening a new business. More than 90% of those businesses, at last look, were continuing to go and grow. This is a tremendous success rate.

The steps and process leading those owners to succeed have been organized for you into this single edition.

We start out helping you to understand yourself in relation to what it takes to be a good entrepreneur. Are you really cut out to own your own business?

Next we help you understand what you are getting into. Why might coffee be a good idea for you?

You will learn how to create a sound business plan.

A good plan is only valuable if you have a process to effectively work that plan. It is called an implementation back-plan.

Several chapters then help you to organize yourself, your business structure and your shop.

Finally we discuss how to actually operate the business, develop products, market yourself, etc.

Along the way, I'll supply you with guides, tools and advice that will help you develop your business to be as successful and efficient as you can make it.

It is my sincere hope that this book proves to be invaluable to you. I have tried to be direct and concise in sharing with you as much information, knowledge and advice as possible from the combined experience of my partners, our broadly experienced staff, and that learned by hundreds of others who have traveled ahead of you on the path you are contemplating.

I also want to encourage you to embark on your entrepreneurial voyage with great enthusiasm. I relish the pleasure of remembering the excitement, joy and pride when we incorporated our first business. We wanted a business that would treat others, as we would like to be treated. Respect for the employees, integrity daily with our own values, and honest value for our customers. We succeeded. You too can do this. You can build a business that reflects you and your values.

Enjoy yourself, create a business you will have fun owning, and I pray that all the powers of the universe work to aid you in your journey.

Perhaps two more bits of information will be helpful and interesting. Where did this name THE Coffee Coach come from? And what is The Coffee Academy?

The word *Coach* was originally used to mean tutor or trainer taking its reference from Stagecoach, which at that time was the fastest mode of transportation. *Coach* in education parlance was an instructor who brought his students along at the fastest pace. We expect this book to save readers about 6 months in start up time and many thousands of investment dollars.

I once had a client named Susan, who, after only half a day of consultation said to me, "David, consultant is really not the most accurate title for you. A consultant advises and influences, a guide leads, a mentor offers wisdom, a friend is supportive, but you are all of these and more. You clarify, enable, educate, empower and motivate. Like a good coach, you inspire people to enthusiastically pursue their dreams and their given potential. You ought to be known as "THE Coffee Coach". I accepted her counsel.

The Coffee Academy is the education arm of Espresso Midwest in Minneapolis. My partners and I built that company into the nations largest and most professionally staffed espresso equipment sales, service and consulting firm by steadfastly pursuing one single purpose, "Our purpose is to do whatever it takes to help clients succeed every day."

This single minded dedication produced numerous helpful training and education aids which are distributed by The Coffee Academy at **emi@espressomidwest.com** or reach me through **www.thecoffeecoach.net**

Introduction

Do You NEED This Book?

If you desire to own and operate any high-yield business, then this first section is integral in assessing your skills and, more importantly, your commitment. Having an interest in opening your own specialty coffee shop is, of course, going to be very helpful in the pages to come. Nevertheless, that interest comes second after a short list of questions that will aid you in gauging your level of commitment. We'll get to some of the precise and challenging questions at the beginning of the first section.

The next section begins answering the questions of why specialty coffees and specialty coffee businesses are still one of the most successful small business opportunities in the food industry. Much of the market research has been compiled and re-researched, and I've put forth the ideas and footprints you'll need to follow to become successful. Of course, most of the work in creating your business will have to be done by you.

Next, and very essential, is a lengthy, thorough discussion on business planning and things that must be done to begin your specialty coffee venture. Much of this information could also be applicable in any self-owned business you might undertake. Estimates, profit and loss, quarterly and yearly projections, employing staff and managers, all of these may seem like busy-work to many emerging entrepreneurs, but I cannot overstress how important it is to formulate a working model before the start of your business venture. You may have heard it before, but it still remains true: "plan your work and work your plan".

The following section offers some how-to's on proprietary site leasing and some forms I've included to make the process easier. Then come the nuts-and-bolts of the businesses operation. What to look for in a roaster, a grinder, an espresso machine, recipes, and possible menu items and so much more.

If you are interested in creating your own coffee business, it's reasonably assumed that you are the type of person that wants to work for yourself. There *are* a number of benefits to working for yourself, not the least of which is that you'll end each and every day with the fruits of *your* labors. Success could lead to financial independence, freedom from bosses and lackadaisical co-workers and, sometimes most importantly, freedom forever from having to share credit for your own work. Self-ownership means that every success, and, yes, every failure, is yours to savor or endure. That is the exciting part of owning any business.

I personally feel that starting a business, which delivers quality products and services while creating both jobs and income for others, is one of the most important social contributions any individual can provide their community.

The road ahead can be a complicated one so pay attention early. Equip yourself with a fresh notebook and a bevy of pencils or pens and let's move ahead into the first section and take a look at that list of questions.

Section I

What Is Required To Be An Entrepreneur?

Chapter One

Do You Really Want To Own A Business?

> Two of life's biggest disappointments are - **not** getting what you wish for and **getting** what you wish for

A dreamer is someone who dreams big dreams, but lacks the initiative to implement them. A visionary sees the future and invests time, money and effort in achieving it. Which are you?

Several years ago, one of my employees coined the term "Davidism" for the little clichéd nuggets of philosophy I tend to drop here and again. I can't seem to resist the temptation to share. "Balance may be the most critical attribute for any new business owner."

Let us examine your sense of balance.

Question One: Do you like working with different kinds of people?

One of the first things you'll notice before opening your doors for business is the awe-inspiring variety of people that exist on this planet. All of them are the people to whom you will eventually trust the hour-to-hour operation of your shiny, new sole source of income. You don't have to like them all, but you do have to know how to deal with them effectively. These are the people who've applied for a job, as well as who make up your customer base. Even the most level tempered may need to learn to be more flexible, and patient and understanding than perhaps you've ever been. Otherwise, you will face the tumultuous scenario of high turnover and slow sales.

Being able to manage, let alone get along with, so many different personality types can be a daunting task for even the most even-tempered of individuals. Added to this, you are now the surrogate parental figure for your new coffee shop family. Can you ask for something to be done? Can you do it in a tactful manner? Can you follow through to make sure it's done? Can you pay or encourage or cajole or bribe them to finish the things there is absolutely no time to finish on your own? Can you…will you get after them until it is? Can you appreciate the differences between individuals while simultaneously creating a process that delivers a consistent level of quality?

Specialty coffee shops are unique when compared to other businesses because, in most cases, a very familial dynamic forms among the people who work there. Coffee shops are comfortable, relaxing and intimate. This is how it must be behind the counter as well, with the equally important priority being the contentment of the customer. Your employees will form bonds, start arguments and share life stories with each other. Occasionally this will lead to feuding and turf wars *inside of your coffee shop!* Maybe they get along perfectly well and there will never be any conflict (…Keep wishing). But, you'll need to be prepared for both scenarios, to allow for some smooth sailing and some rough seas, while still keeping the entire staff focused on giving every customer professional service.

Your job here, as the lead worker, is to settle disputes, maintain order and espouse diplomacy and, in most other cases, act as an authority figure to your new batch of foster kids-and foster adults. When your employees feel cared for, when they are happy, this is when you get the highest quality of work and devotion from them. I've found that demonstrating to employees that they are number one, teaches them how to make customers feel number one. No amount of money can construct a dedicated, efficient work force the way that a personal, one-on-one relationship can. Of course, a competitive wage never hurts.

In addition to these many challenges, you will be called upon to make every single one of your customers feel needed, special and happy. Yes, that's every single one. Even though this is the ideal, it's not completely possible. Don't beat yourself up just keep at it. As important as your employees are to you, you won't be able to afford them for very long if your clientele ever feels alienated. Finding this balance is one of the more complex tasks you have before you, in this or in any business.

Question Two: Am I Strong Enough To Start My Own Business?

How do you feel?

An eighty-hour workweek is not uncommon for a new business owner, and it is more the rule than the exception. Your physical condition is a significant consideration before you decide to strike out on your own. How's your back? How's your heart? How're your feet? Even in your most moderate sales hours you will be running around cleaning this, preparing that and moving that stack of heavy stuff over here into a new stack of heavy stuff over there, or asking, telling or calling for someone else to. Are you the type of person to work this hard and enjoy doing it?

How do you feel?

Your mental capacity is also a point upon which you need to give yourself an honest self-examination. How positive is your attitude? What about the breakfast/lunch/ dinner/ after-the-show rushes? Can you handle those customer free hours in which your employees, after cleaning the entire store form top to bottom, eat up your operating capital *and the muffins* while they stare vacantly at the wall? Can you focus more on growth than on cost? Can you maintain a calm and tranquil state of mind when your computer crashes and your quarterly taxes are due? Can you maintain your serenity when your employee, the one who is supposed to relieve you after you've spent ten hours on your feet, calls in with a sniffle and decides to take the day off? All these things, and more, *are going to happen*. Sorry, but there's no question about it. All of this and more will happen. So, before you have to call in the Happy Van, take stock of your personality strengths and weaknesses. Wishful thinking never helped anyone during a short-staffed commuter rush.

How do you feel?

Given any of the above-mentioned scenarios, how are you likely to respond? Are you the type of person who will quietly shake your head, tell the person who just called to take the day off to relax and take care of the sniffles and tough out the rest of the day yourself? Are you the type of person who will shake your head, mutter a quick "Why me?" and get back to work? Or, are you the type of person who will verbally chastise your employee, order them out of bed immediately and then sit stewing in righteous indignation while you melt the door practicing the look you're going to give that little...? And then, what do you do when he or she still doesn't show, and goes to work for your competition? So, do yourself a favor and think about it beforehand. How *do* you feel? How will you react? And, how is your blood pressure?

Question Three: How is your support system?

Since we've already established that you are the new, if temporary, parent to a diverse, green crew of individuals who need you to solve their moment to moment torments and anxieties while simultaneously solving all of the problems and needs of the customer: who do you turn to when the pressure builds up?

Whether it's a spouse, partner, friend or family member, not enough can be said for having someone to turn to when you need a hand, in any walk of life, but more specifically, in owning your own enterprise. The daily pressures that you will face could seem overwhelming even if, in some sense, they actually aren't. Don't be afraid to ask for guidance, for the layperson's opinion, or even just a little help. You should never feel the need to be a super hero. Draw the help you need from the people you know that are most able to furnish it.

You will experience many successes. You'll see days when your sales soar, days when you figure out how to repair a machine that has stopped and days when you lead one of your employees to a breakthrough. You may fail to enjoy your successes if they're not shared with others. These and many other successes can be shared with your loved ones and support group to contribute to the overall enjoyment of ownership and accomplishment. You'll be surprised at how many people will want to share in and reinforce your excitement.

With every new business venture, an honest and factual examination of your finances is of paramount importance to your future. How long can you go without a paycheck? How much are you willing to spend to make your dream a success? What will you do if there isn't enough money to make ends meet? Who might be able to loan you the money if absolutely necessary? What will your system of support be willing to endure? What corners can you cut without jeopardizing the product *in any way*? What can you make or make do or do without?

Question Four: Can you do everything?

Management is eventually responsible for everything that takes place under the scope of the business, for better or for worse. That just happens to be the way it goes.

From payroll to floor mopping, it falls to you to oversee every tiny event and occurrence under the roof of your new business, or at the least, being able to perform it yourself. Some minutes seem endless, while other days and weeks just seem to fly past, leaving you wondering where the time went and why you're suddenly feeling years older. Can you keep up?

Knowledge is the key to understanding your limitations. Are you going to be able to learn and do all the different things required of your new business?

Are you going to be able to compensate for the knowledge you lack when difficult situations arrive? Are you the type of person who can ask for help and delegate effectively or do you need to handle every task yourself? At some point you are going to have to hire, train, supervise and motivate your employees. Do you know what to show them?

Hopefully you've looked deep inside of yourself and found a stronger, more organized person than you'd thought was there. If you still have doubts, however, don't worry about it. By the time you've finished this book you should be able to come back and take this self-test again. You should have a far more comfortable outcome.

At the conclusion of each key segment, I will encourage you to reflect upon what you have just read.

Having read the previous pages, do you feel more enthused about becoming your own boss? Were you forced to say no to any of the questions I've asked?

Is it clear to you that every business needs a strong leader? Will you provide that leadership? Whom will you call upon to help if you cannot?

> Nature abhors a vacuum and will undertake any action to fill it. Get there first.

Chapter Two:

Assessing Your Opportunity

What are you going to do? What do you know about the marketplace?

Often repeated and more often than not misunderstood is the expression: *"Build a better mousetrap and the world will beat a path to your door"*. However, you may derive more insight from the expression: *"Find a void and FILL IT"*. You can build a successful business if you:

- Find out who needs your business and its products.

- Understand what products and services your future customers use now and find a way to convey how much better and more attractive your products are.

- Learn what they'll buy and how much of it they want.

- Recognize who your competition is and <u>who it isn't</u>. What is your competition likely to do in response to your entrance into the market and how you'll be able to overcome the backlash from the competition?

There are several more questions that you'll need to answer. Run into the other room and grab a notebook and a pen. First, the *"who's."*

- Who needs or desires your product or service...now, how did you get your answer? Was it just wishful thinking or was it based on cold, hard facts and objective assessment? We'll go into specifics a little later.

- Who are your customers? Where do they live? Where do they work? Where do they shop? What do they buy when they shop?

- Who is your target demographic-your *new* customers? What age group do you want to target? What is the education level of this group? How much money do they make? How will you attract them to your business? What do they want and how much are they willing to spend for it?

- Who is your realistic competition? How will you set yourself apart from them? What makes your business different and how will you market yourself to accentuate these differences?

- Who should you *market* yourself toward? How will they find you? Will they return? Why or why not? How can you stay in their mind?

- How can you protect yourself against a competitor stealing your customers-and your employees? Remember to "Think Quality" in your service and in your product. Also keep in mind, the first precept of this business is to always be inviting, to treat each customer like a favored guest you are entertaining.

Now, the "W*hat's*." Let's try to more accurately identify the questions specific to your understanding of your *products* and your *marketplace*.

The first responsibility of management is to make a profit, because without it, everything else involved just stops. However, you'll need to set prices that are profitable yet reasonably competitive. There will always be the temptation to charge discounted prices for certain products to help increase your cash flow or attract new customers. This is a point that must be emphatically hammered home: "*When you stop adding value, you will stop succeeding*". Most customers know when they are paying too much for a given item and they *will* resent it. But, if the prices are too low, your business will have to struggle. *"When a business becomes focused on cost instead of value and elects to compete on price at the expense of quality, it has already begun to go out of business."*

> A *Davidism*: The best advice? Price your menu fairly and buy your quality wisely. When you stop adding value, you will stop succeeding.

This is yet another balancing act that would serve you to analyze.

- What exactly is the product and service you expect to be paid for?
- What materials and supplies will you need to make the product?
- From whom are you going to purchase your supplies?
- What research do you need to do in order to find the best supplier?
- What do you need to know to help you build a trusting relationship with your supplier?
- What will make your product cost effective?
- What if a disaster should strike either your supplier or yourself, do you have a back up plan to recover your business productivity?
- What publications should you subscribe to or what groups should you belong to that will aid you in your business?
- What do leaders in your industry say about the future of the industry? And if you don't know-find out! In this particular instance, the Specialty Coffee Association of America (www.SCAA.org) is a great place to start.

As you read this book, check back and see if your answers are the same or if you've been able to define, refine and redefine parts of your answers. This collection of notes might be a good reference for the later creation of the actual business plan.

- Your local city planning department or your landlord should have current demographic profiles.
- The SCAA can provide industry trends.
- Your state's Small Business Advisory Center may be helpful.
- Your personal observations, foot traffic counts and neighborhood surveys will prove invaluable.

TIME OUT

<u>Team Huddle</u>

Design your business well and you need build it only once. The reverse to this usually sounds like "Why is there never time to do it right, but always time to do it over?"

A man began remodeling his space with a basic idea sketched out in his head as to what he was trying to build, but with no other planning. One day the health department came in and told him he had installed the wrong wall material. Furthermore, he would have to tear it off and do it right.

Another day, he discovered the used display case he had purchased did not meet health department standards, and the new one he would have to buy was four inches longer than the old. Now he was forced to tear out half of his brand new counter to make the new cooler fit.

He spent his money as he went along and because he wasn't following a plan or a budget he ran out of money. This man was opening a coffee bar and ice cream shop. Would you like to guess what he hadn't yet purchased when he ran out of money? …His coffee equipment and ice cream freezer display, of course. So, he bought both of them used.

The first month, his espresso machine failed, and we found the boiler half filled with scale. He decided he could not afford to rent a replacement machine while we repaired his, so customers couldn't buy espresso drinks those days.

The 4th of July parade went right in front of his store and he planned to capture several thousand in sales that day. The morning of the parade, he arrived to find his used freezer and display had stopped working overnight. All of his ice cream was destroyed, repairs were going to cost over $3,000 and he had nothing to sell for the big parade day and holiday weekend. Disheartened, he closed the door and never returned.

Chapter Three

Planning the Approach

Really, what's the point of all this?

So, let's speak to the *"How's"*.

> # Plan your work
> # And
> # Work your plan

Every new business needs extensive *planning* and *organization*. Remember, how you plan and organize your business, in your head and on paper, will greatly influence its ultimate success or failure.

- How are you going to manage your company? Your finances, your employees, your downtimes?

- How will you go about marketing, sales and location selections?

- How will you structure your business? Will you incorporate? An LLC, an LLP, or Sole Ownership? What are the advantages and disadvantages of each? What are all of these abbreviations?

As you can see, the possibilities are quite numerous. So, take more notes, and by the end of this book you will have a successful business plan. Many a successful business has been started on notebooks and napkins.

Understanding Yourself Is The First Key

Some people have a very difficult time managing their own behavior and activities. It is imperative to learn how it is that you manage yourself before you ever take the steps of hiring and managing others. How are you supposed to teach yourself such an intangible and unreachable concept? Besides the basic idea of just getting your stuff and ideas and plans and appointments *organized*, here is an approach I have found very successful in my business dealings:

An accountant once told me to look upon myself as a limited and finite supply of energy. He said: *"Your objective is to spend your energy where and how it will be the most efficient for both your personal and business objectives"*. Then he suggested the following:

*"Create a list of the things you like to do and that you're good at on one side of a page and things you do like, but are not good at on the other. Take a second page and list things you **do not** like to do but do well and also those you do not like but that you know are important to your objectives."*

This will begin to prepare you to prioritize your time and also decide the type of skills you need to find in employees and advisors.

Where am I supposed to find the time?

Dr. Steven Covey, successful business author, writes: *"You have all the time there is. How you spend it is called priorities."*

Accept the inevitability that you have three, and only three, levels of priority. "A", "B" and "C". Now, "A" priorities are those things that are essential to the profitability and smooth operation of your business *and can only be done adequately by the owner.* "A" priorities are sometimes not very much fun, but these "A" priorities cannot be accomplished by anyone but you. Marketing, Budgeting and Training are definitely "A" priorities in the first years.

"B" priorities are the other important activities that you may enjoy performing. In most cases, these can be completed by just about anyone that works for you. Product preparation and customer relations are considered "B" priorities. Make sure you don't allow "B" priorities to supercede "A" priorities, or they will eventually come back to haunt you.

Sadly, "C" priorities are often a bit of a pain in the neck, no one wants to do them, and often they are ignored. Cleaning the sidewalks and mopping the floors are sometimes viewed as "C" priorities. Nevertheless, these are seen, by many customers, as the most important tasks that you and your employees can execute. Keep in mind, while doing these chores, that Orderliness and Cleanliness are important to the smooth running of any business, but critical in the foodservice industry to achieve positive customer impressions.

Hopefully, you can learn to delegate these responsibilities and oversee their proper completion. Just remember one simple thing: never, ever make an employee do something that you yourself would not do. Why should they if you never will? Yes, that means that every once in a while, you too will have to clean a toilet. Sorry about that, but it's good for morale. Serve your employees well, and they will serve your customers well.

Every priority listed above has its own changing level of importance from minute to minute throughout the day. You must learn to differentiate the significance, impacts and appropriate times for each and every A, B and C task.

When is it time to hire a manager?

That is a very good question. *When it's in the best interest of the business* is the very good answer to that very good question.

It is also a question that you cannot answer until you are comfortable with the independent running of your company while you are off somewhere else. Off-site. Out of sight. You're not there to place a band-aid on a cut finger *or put out a fire!* It may take several emotionally scarring episodes before you've properly trained someone who will perform management tasks with sufficient skill and composure to put your mind at ease. Make sure that you not only have a cell phone but that you are able, over time, to turn it off.

31

Take a look at your staff and decide if there is at least one person in your new family that can be trusted to take on the additional responsibilities of management. Are they mature? Do they have more experience? Are they more interested? You'll have to decide what qualifications make one employee a more attractive choice for management over another. There is a lot to be said for experience, and for education, but much more to be said for self-confidence and for positive attitude.

Now that you've taken a long, hard look at your new family, do you think it might be a good idea to hire one more person that has management experience? Perhaps. You'll know when it's time to think about it.

Once you've found your new manager, be sure to pay them enough to maintain their pride in the job and give them incentives that make them feel like a minor partner in your new enterprise. A sense of ownership will go a long way toward giving your manager a feeling of satisfaction when the company does well. Remember the three "A's"- Attitude Affects All.

This is as good a place as any for a reflective pause.

Questions:

- How do you feel?
- Is your enthusiasm and confidence growing?
- Have you learned some things about yourself that you might not have previously valued or appreciated?

TIME OUT

Team Huddle

A Success Story

Plan your work. Have a realistic budget. Design your business so it is efficient to construct and efficient to operate. Success very seldom happens for people who are ill-prepared, too lazy to do things well or chaotic.

Success happens more easily to those who think clearly, plan well, work hard, respect their customers, employees and suppliers and remain excited about the business they are running.

While it may often be easier to learn from someone else's mistakes, here is a success story I just love to tell because she got it right the first time around.

She arrived for our first meeting with a 3-inch 3-hole folder with about 8 dividers. She had been collecting ideas and doing research and organizing the answers in this folder for several weeks. Two weeks after our first meeting, she returned with a draft of a business plan about 80% finished. When we finished working out the numbers she was very excited.

The next time we met, she had a signed lease and had hired a designer to create drawings and layout after she and I established her final menu and equipment list. Our friend also sought the help of a councilperson to petition for a variance to allow her to put in a drive up window.

The day she opened, her store looked exactly as I had envisioned it from her very clear description and the drawings I had seen. The menu was well presented. The local press had done a broad weekend article on her so on Monday morning the store was filled with interested townsfolk.

Ninety days later she was able to open the drive up window, and this gave the paper an excuse for another feature story. The public rushed to this great new convenience and she had her first $1,000 day a full six months ahead of her business plan.

This client had become very clear in her mind about her purpose and objectives. She wrote a clear and detailed plan. She hired professionals to guide her. Because of the orderly implementation approach, she was not overwhelmed, frustrated or emotionally exhausted, but rather was excited and enthused when she opened. The public simply responded, with their money.

Section II

The Coffee Opportunity

Why is Specialty Coffee so Special?

> **Coffee is the most common drink enjoyed worldwide in family, social, business or political gatherings.**

Chapter Four

Why coffee? Why now?

Is coffee even the best idea for me?

This may be a good place to speak about the growth of the coffee industry as seen by these opinions of some industry leaders, taken from Fancy Food, Nov. 98: *"The trend of younger coffee drinkers will continue. Drinking espresso or specialty coffee is the cool in-thing"*. Joanne Shaw, Coffee Beanery Ltd.

"Darker roast coffees will gain market share as roasters become more proficient at these difficult blends". Bruce Mullin, CBI Inc.

According to industry association studies, since '94 approximately 47% of the American population consumed an average of 2 cups a day, with a 50% rise in espresso drinking and 9% more drinking cappuccino. In '98 daily consumption rose to three cups a day. Yes, that's three actual cups per day. Upscale professionals, educators, medical workers and students are the highest consumers of gourmet coffees. People who drink specialty coffee and espresso-based drinks are often in a higher financial bracket in comparison to non-consumers. People are living longer and kicking their kids out-so what are they going to do with all that disposable time and income? Inviting coffee houses continue to increase in popularity, but all your competitors are after the same market share. What makes you different? *You are going to be better prepared.*

Coffee is a fun industry!

Imagine professional business types stopping by *your* cart on the way in and on the way out of their office building. Doctors and interns and nurses and medical aids and clerical workers will be using their disposable income to get specialty drinks at *your* hospital kiosk. Visualize students sitting outside of *your* leased site at the student union, spending their parents' money getting triple shots during finals week. Meanwhile, across town, the neighborhood is hitting *your* coffee house to listen to music and to visit with friends, as the local teens are hooked up to *your* internet stations at $4 an hour, sipping on one of those huge mugs of Mocha, paying for re-fills and tipping your competent baristas. Coffee entrepreneurs clearly know what demographic they're after, how to attract attention and satisfy people so that they return often.

Coffee is fun because you are dealing all day with interesting people and using common sense to make them feel welcome and special.

A new coffee business is affordable!

A simple *cart start-up* might cost between 20-30K and could easily make a gross of $75,000 to $200,000 *in the first year.* The average specialty bar makes 40-60% gross margin overall, selling upwards of 200 cups/day from $1.50 to $4.00 a cup. Potential realized profits from 35-75K net/year.

A full scale coffee house of say 1500 square feet may cost between $50,000 and $150,000 and produce revenues of between $250,000 and $500,000 annually. Compare that to costs for a simple restaurant where hardly anyone can carry out a successful start-up with less than half a million dollars.

This is not rocket science. You don't need an advanced degree. The industry requires less capital and produces more return than many other industries, so you can take home extra well-earned benefits from your efforts. If you can run a dishwasher, you can operate an espresso machine. If you can use an electric can opener, you can grind coffee and espresso. If you prefer to not do either, you can find and hire someone who does.

A coffee business, like so many others, requires attention to three basic factors, just like any business, you need to pay attention to details, stay focused on making the customer feel special, and treat your employees with respect.

Coffee Is Popular!

In cities like Seattle, New York, San Francisco, Minneapolis and Miami, there are plentiful numbers of espresso/coffee houses, carts and kiosks in the major metropolitan areas. You'd be hard pressed to find an office building, hospital lobby or city block without one. However, and more to the point, the specialty coffee market in these big cities is nowhere near saturated. Far from it, really. Italy, for example, has more than one hundred coffee houses to every one in these larger American cities.

Coffee, as a business, has yet to see itself max out any marketplace. On a recent visit to Seattle I happened to see a sign that read: *"Last Chance For Coffee For 50 Feet"*. No other statement can more accurately reflect the openness of coffee and espresso as a marketable business.

There really is no adequate way to convey the irresistible number of possibilities this product has in America. It would take more pages…than I care to write or you may care to read to spell out everything, and let's face it, you need to do most of the research in your area to decide how *you* will proceed. I will discuss this more in the coming section.

So; let's understand the two major coffee plants as we know them.

Robusta.

Robusta coffees are the dominant presence in the worldwide coffee market. The robusta plant can grow in almost any warm climate, at almost any altitude. Needless to say, this makes the robusta a very hearty plant. Robusta plants are easier to grow, require less attention, and will harvest almost four times versus one harvest by the arabica plant. In addition to being inexpensive, robusta beans have almost twice the caffeine of arabica beans. They do, however lack the distinctive flavor and aroma profile preferred by discriminating consumers. Almost every common, store-brand shelf-coffee is made primarily from robusta beans.

Arabica.

Arabica beans deliver the vivid and distinguished taste characteristics that are somewhat lacking in Robusta varieties. For this reason, arabica beans are considered superior to the robusta. Arabica beans are much more susceptible to disease and can only be grown along the equator between the Tropic of Cancer and the Tropic of Capricorn. They are only able to sustain their proper harvest rates at higher altitudes. Most arabica plantations are planted on mountainsides making the harvest that much more difficult to execute.

All in all, with smaller harvest, demanding rainfall needs, soil conditions, labor needs, hand picking and on and on, it's a small wonder that arabica beans cost considerably more than robusta beans. But, it is precisely this superior taste and distinguishing profile of the arabica that have fueled the specialty coffee industry's growth within the past twenty years.

I often tell people the heart of this business is entertaining and educating the customers. Learning more about coffee is as easy as paying a visit to your local specialty coffee roaster or reading trade publications like *Fresh Cup, Gourmet Retailer, Tea & Coffee*, etc. You may also contact the Specialty Coffee Association of America (SCAA).

In an effort to help explain why coffee is so special, let's take a look at the long and tumultuous history that coffee has fought its way through. Maybe this will help you understand how coffee has changed the lives of the people it has touched and the cultures it has altered. Coffee is now as American as Apple pie, and this section can illustrate that Americans have the same insatiable appetite for coffee as they have for the local pizza.

Chapter Five

A Brief History Of Coffee

> **The history of coffee is filled with a romantic mix of myth and fact.**

There is only one commodity traded more widely throughout the world than coffee: Oil (Black Gold, Texas Tea).

Specialty Coffee is fast becoming the cornerstone accessory in the world of gourmet food. Expected market growth rates show only continued and expanded customer demand. As the consumers become further educated with the names and locations of plantation coffees, and as they become more familiar with the unique tastes that are specific to the coffee growing regions, your customers will quietly demand that you know a little something about what it is that they are buying. But also, if they don't know specialty coffee just yet, you'll have the chance to educate your customers a bit. I'm sure they'll love to hear the info, and it will bring them back in for more.

The history of coffee is vague at best, but let me see if I can put some order to it. The story of coffee is a rich mixture of both myth and fact. In reality, the speculation and the storytelling make the whole truth far more entertaining.

A North African goatherd named Kaldi first noticed the effect of coffee beans on behavior. He noticed that the goats became hyperactive after eating the red "cherries" from a certain plant whenever they changed pastures. His curiosity piqued, Kaldi decided to try a few, and quite enjoyed the results.

The story continues: A monk happened by and scolded him for "partaking of the devil's fruit." However, other monks soon discovered that this fruit from the shiny green plant helped them stay awake for their prayers.

Legend also gives us another name for coffee or "mocha." An Arabian monk named Omar was banished with his followers into the desert for preaching Christianity. In hunger and desperation, Omar and his friends boiled and ate the fruit from an unknown shiny green plant. Not only did this "soup" save the lives of the exiles, but also the residents of the nearby town, Mocha, took their survival as a religious sign. The plant and its beverage were named Mocha to honor this event. Mocha ultimately grew into one of the major coffee shipping ports.

One early use for coffee would have little appeal today. The Galla tribe of Ethiopia used coffee, but not as a drink. They would wrap the beans in animal fat and use this sludge as a portable food source when they were off harassing and raiding their neighbors.

Then the Turks, God bless 'em, were the first to make coffee as a drink, often adding spices such as clove, cinnamon, cardamom and anise to the brew. The flavored coffees of today are not such a new idea.

Coffee was introduced much later to countries beyond the Middle East whose inhabitants believed it to be a delicacy and attempted to guard its secret from the rest of the region. The government forbade transportation of the plant out of the Muslim nations. The actual spread of coffee was started illegally. One Arab named Baba Budan smuggled beans into the mountains near Mysore, India, and began one of the first real coffee plantations.

Coffee was believed by some Christians to be the devil's drink. Pope Vincent VIII heard this and decided to taste it before he banished it. He enjoyed it so much he baptized it, saying, "Coffee is so delicious it would be a pity to let the infidels have exclusive use of it." Thus, with papal dispensation, millions of the faithful were permitted to imbibe the heavenly brew.

Flavoring has been added to coffee in numerous societies for hundreds of years. Only the method of adding it has changed. Modern technology allows us to have many more flavors. Sugar, Cardamom, Cinnamon, Nutmeg, Vanilla, Licorice and others are widely used.

A brief chronology of coffee development includes:

In the beginning: Members of the Galla tribe in Ethiopia get an energy boost when they eat a certain berry, ground up and mixed with animal fat.

800 A.D.: Kaldi notices the excited behavior of his goats.

1000 A.D.: Arab traders bring coffee back to their homeland and cultivate the plant for the first time on plantations. They also began to boil the beans; creating a drink they call "qahwa" (literally, that which prevents sleep).

1453: Coffee is introduced to Constantinople by Ottoman Turks. The world's first coffee shop, Kiva Han, opens there in 1475. Turkish law makes it legal for a woman to divorce her husband if he fails to provide her with her daily quota of coffee.

1511: Khair Beg, the corrupt governor of Mecca, tries to ban coffee for fear that its influence might foster opposition to his rule. The Sultan of Cairo overturns the ban and sends word that coffee is sacred. The governor was executed.

1600: Coffee, introduced to the West by Italian traders, grabs attention in high places. In Italy, Pope Clement VIII is urged by his advisers to consider that favorite drink of the Ottoman Empire part of the infidel threat. However, he decides to "baptize" it instead, making it an acceptable Christian beverage.

1607: Captain John Smith helps to found the colony of Virginia at Jamestown. It's believed that he introduced coffee to North America.

1645: First coffeehouse opens in Italy.

1652: First coffeehouse opens in England. Coffee houses multiply and become such popular forums for learned and not so learned - discussion that they are dubbed "penny universities" (a penny being the price of a cup of coffee).

1668: Coffee replaces beer as New York's City's favorite breakfast drink.

1668: Edward Lloyd's coffeehouse opens in England and is frequented by merchants and maritime insurance agents. Eventually it becomes Lloyd's of London, the best-known insurance organization in the world.

1672: First coffeehouse opens in Paris.

1675: The Turkish Army surrounds Vienna. Franz George Kolschitzky, a Viennese who had lived in Turkey, slips through the enemy lines to lead relief forces to the city. The fleeing Turks leave behind sacks of "dry black fodder" that Kolschitzky recognizes as coffee. He claims it as his reward and opens central Europe's first coffee house. He also establishes the habit of refining the brew by filtering out the grounds, sweetening it, and adding a dash of milk.

1675: The first coffee shop opens in the new world in Boston, MA.

1690: With a coffee plant smuggled out of the Arab port of Mocha, the Dutch become the first to transport and cultivate coffee commercially, in Ceylon and in their East Indian colony - Java, source of the brew's nickname.

1696: The opening of *The Kings Arms*, the first coffee house in New York.

1713: The Dutch unwittingly provide Louis XIV of France with a coffee bush whose descendants eventually produce the entire Western coffee industry.

1721: First coffee house opens in Berlin.

1723: French naval officer Gabriel Mathieu du Clieu steals a seedling and transports it to Martinique. Within 50 years an official survey records 19 million coffee trees on Martinique. Eventually, 90 percent of the world's coffee spreads from this plant.

1727: The Brazilian coffee industry gets its start when Lieutenant colonel Francisco de Melo Palheta is sent by government to arbitrate a border dispute between the French and the Dutch colonies in Guiana. Not only does he resolve the dispute, but also strikes up a secret relationship with the wife of French Guiana's governor. Although France guarded its New World coffee plantations to prevent cultivation from spreading, the lady said farewell to Palheta with a garland in which she hid cuttings and fertile seeds of coffee.

1732: Johann Sebastian Bach composes his Coffee-Cantata. Partly an ode to coffee and partly a sneer at the German movement to thwart women from drinking coffee (it was thought to make them sterile), the cantata includes the aria, "Ah! How sweet coffee tastes! Lovelier than a thousand kisses, sweeter far than muscatel wine! I must have my coffee." (A rough translation, to be sure)

1773: The Boston Tea Party makes drinking coffee a patriotic act in new America.

1775: Prussia's Frederick the Great tries to block imports of green coffee, as Prussia's wealth is drained. Mass public demonstrations change his mind.

1886: Former wholesale grocer Joel Cheek names his popular coffee blend "Maxwell House," after the hotel in Nashville, TN where it's served.

Early 1900's: In Germany, afternoon coffee becomes a standard occasion. The derogatory term "Kaffee Klatch" is coined to describe women's gossip at these affairs. It has since broadened as a phrase to mean relaxed conversation in general.

1900: Hills Bros. begins packing roast coffee in vacuum tins, spelling the end of the all-pervading local roasting shops and coffee mills.

1901: Japanese-American chemist Satori Kato of Chicago invents the first soluble "instant" coffee.

1903: German coffee importer Ludwig Roselius turned a batch of ruined coffee beans over to scientists, who perfected the process of removing caffeine from the beans without too badly destroying the flavor. He markets this new "un-caff" under the brand name "Sanka."

1906: George Constant Washington, an English chemist living in Guatemala, notices a powdery brown condensation forming on the spout of his silver coffee carafe. After experimentation, he creates the first mass-produced instant coffee called *Red-E*.

1914: After the assassination of Archduke Franz Ferdinand, Europe explodes into the First World War. The demand for coffee on both sides of the war causes coffee plantations to radically expand the growing of Robusta coffee. Given its high caffeine content and high yield, robusta remained the dominant bean sold for the next 85 years.

1920: Prohibition goes into effect in United States. Coffee sales soar.

1923: Sanka is introduced to the United States.

1936: Orlando Simonelli first employs the electronic pump in espresso machines.

1940: The United States was importing almost 70% of the world's coffee crop.

1942: During W.W.II, American soldiers are issued instant Maxwell House coffee in their c-ration kits. Widespread hoarding back home leads to coffee rationing.

1945: In Italy, Achilles Gaggia invents the piston espresso machine.

1971: Starbucks opens its first store in Seattle's Pike Place public market.

Isn't it interesting, as you read the timeline, to note how the spread in the popularity of coffee so closely parallels the major wars of the last one thousand years? For more information on the history of coffee I suggest reading *The World of Caffeine: The Science and Culture of the World's Most Popular Drug* by Bennett Alan Weinberg and Bonnie K. Baler and *Uncommon Grounds* by Mark Pendergrast.

<table>
<tr><td>

Build your business
around you, not the other
way around

</td><td>

Chapter Six

Coffee Businesses and How
To Choose One

</td></tr>
</table>

Before we get into discussions of financing, I think it would be best for you to do a little sightseeing. I'm going to break this chapter into three sections to help make my point about the subject of WHERE. Then you'll be able to sight see with specific questions banging around inside your head. So, let's address the types of stores, and possible locations that would prove most beneficial for each.

1. Coffee Carts.

The most wonderful thing about owning a coffee cart is the portability of your operation. After all the time you'll spend putting together the most comprehensive start up package that you can afford, if you find yourself suffering from lackluster business traffic, you can always pick up and move on to another location.

You see; carts are entirely self-contained business units. Your potable water is stored on board in refillable tanks, your waste is contained in another removable tank that can be dumped at the end of your business day. Carts are regularly wired from an external power source to a central circuit breaker located within the cart where you can connect the cords to your equipment. Admittedly, you'll need more than just power, which is why proper and comprehensive location scouting is very important to your mobility and your success.

Event catering is also a nice alternative when you own a coffee cart. All you need is mode of transportation to and from the event. Coffee Catering, when handled correctly, can be a very lucrative business in its own right. The field of possibilities is nearly endless. From sports arenas to weddings, portability allows you flexibility. Flexibility equals profitability.

Arenas and convention centers are the perfect semi-permanent home for a cart-based business. When the game or show is over you will roll your cart away for storage until you roll it out again for another event. Convention centers are filled throughout the week with tired travelers from home and abroad who will appreciate the convenience of your delicious coffee products. There are often multiple separate events taking place inside the walls of a convention center and all you need is access to electricity to operate your cart. Arenas and convention centers are heavily wired for this very reason. Access to power is not often as difficult as you might think at first.

2. Kiosks

One of the nice things about owning a kiosk happens before you open for business. Kiosks are usually, and I do stress usually, less expensive than store fronts to start up, and not nearly as difficult to staff. Depending on where you finally decide to locate your kiosk, rent is often also much less expensive and should you decide to relocate, just bring the whole thing with you.

Keep in mind that carts and kiosks are very similar in that they can fit into and operate in many locations. However, while you can put a cart anywhere, kiosks are a semi-permanent installation in most cases. After you find a location for your kiosk, you must negotiate its size, style and rent with the owners of the building where you plan to be located. Do some quick mental marketing about the areas in which you might be able to place one.

Hospitals are a very good location for a kiosk coffee shop. Your clientele is split between the captive staff at the hospital and the always-abundant patients of hospital itself and the guests of the patients. Shopping malls also offer an attractive profitability quotient for the kiosk proprietor. Noting that hospitals usually charge less per square foot than a shopping mall easily sums up the difference between these two spaces. Malls have wider fluctuations in traffic flow, and your clientele is a bit more subdued and less demanding in a hospital.

However, concerning shopping malls, even the busier ones, your choice of location is imperative. The mall management's willingness to give you space in one of the higher trafficked areas will depend on a few different circumstances:

1. **Design**: What do you want your store design to look and feel like? What will make it attractive to the public? In some hospitals as well as in many older malls, these are not important considerations for the landlord. While a hospital is usually self-sufficient, many older malls are just happy to lease the space to keep the cash flowing in. Newer and more stylistic malls of the present, and of the future, will generate much more traffic, but may also require a significant amount of conformity from you, your store and your staff.

2. **Environment**: How well will your kiosk design blend with the area you wish to operate? As the size, scale and theme of America's malls change and develop, more and more emphasis will be placed on how well you contribute to the overall feel. How will having your kiosk in the middle of an aisle way add or subtract from the ambiance of that part of the mall? Unfortunately, this all depends on the arbitrary opinions and ever-changing tastes of mall management. You may find that your kiosk design will change radically from its conception to its actualization the more you are forced to take input from the powers that be.

3. **Rent**: Buying products in a mall is rarely, if ever, inexpensive. So goes the cost of doing business in a mall. As you know, the mall property is, in and of itself, a business. That business takes its primary cash flow from the rent collected from the businesses within. Granted, the easiest time to negotiate

a rent structure is during the initial construction of the mall itself, but this will almost never be a bankable option. Management companies are more willing to negotiate when the mall does not yet have a full contingent of renters. Employing the help of a business or real estate lawyer is *always* a good idea.

Colleges and Universities are also prime locations for the home of your cart or kiosk. There will always be a large contingent of customers, i.e. students, teachers and staff, who will crave your product and frequent your establishment. Given that the majority of specialty coffee drinkers fall between the ages of 18 and 45, colleges and universities are frequently a good bet for a successful site. Add into consideration the total number of college students that are always looking for work and you should never have a problem re-staffing to meet turnover.

As tempting as it may be to set up your new cart or kiosk in the hallowed halls of higher education, there are a few things to ponder.

```
A Davidism:
Competing on
    price
 instead of
 quality can
 put you out
 of business
  quickly.
```

- It is often expensive to rent space on campus. Quite a lot of businesses want the very space you're looking for.

- Negotiating for a prime location will take place with people who often do not use or understand your product.

- Colleges and universities are also a business. Unlike malls that want both conformity and cash, campus management usually just wants the cash.

- Students usually care more about the quality of product over the appearance of your kiosk. What you save in set up costs may be displaced by the need to up the cost and quality of your primary product line.

- The simple advice is for institutions of higher learning as well as all sites is as follows: "*Always Serve the Best Coffee-or- Never, Ever, Serve Bad Coffee*". College age kids are the first American generation to have grown up into a world of high quality coffee. Even if you charge only fifty-seven cents a cup, cheap coffee will sink your business faster than a torpedo into a dinghy. There is no need to ever compete on prices. Make product quality and service be the basis of your competition.

Office buildings are yet another alternative to the previously mentioned site choices. People with money, in a hurry, who need to keep up with the more and more demanding world of business, can always use a good cup of java.

One of my favorite innovations in the world of specialty coffee is borrowed from the parking lot photo booth. Drive-through coffee outlets are proving to be some of the most advantageous site alternatives in existence. Why didn't anyone think of it before? Many new coffee shop owners have found that life at the end of the lot is a much less expensive, high "traffic," very profitable change from retail storefront-based shops. There will be more on permanent storefronts later.

In the meantime, below is a partial list of acceptable locations that could prove to become your location of choice. See if any of these suggestions mesh with the locations you've considered.

- Sports Arenas
- Shopping Malls
- Office Buildings
- Colleges and Universities
- Light Rail Stations
- Train Stations
- Hospitals

- Hotels
- Busy Parking Lots
- Grocery Stores
- Book Stores
- Lumber and Home Improvement Stores
- High End Audio and Computer Outlets
- Retail Stores
- Health Food Markets
- Farmer's Markets
- State Fairs and Festivals
- Flea Markets
- Swap Meets
- Churches
- High Schools
- Space Stations

The possibilities are really almost endless.

3. Storefronts

Storefronts are your preferred option if you want to unleash all of your imagination into your shop design. For a number of reasons, storefronts will almost always cost more to set up than carts or kiosks. One reason might be because of certain building lease options while another might be because of the amount of internal and external construction you've projected. For some people, the higher cost is an unimportant consideration when compared to the freedom and joy of building their own design up from an idea. Within reasonable parameters, you will be allowed to create the specific image and feel of your coffee shop's anticipated personality.

You should plan for your storefront to be around quite a while. While owning the land and guiding the construction are ideal, it is not always the most cost-effective or realistic option.

Rent is the major consideration when you decide to lease space from a mall, mini-mall, strip mall or the independent standing building. You're the one who needs to do your homework here. Begin by staking out the locations that you think would make a good home to your business. You will need to spend several hours counting the foot and/or auto traffic past the door to your intended spot. You may need to count both if it's relevant.

Since you've already decided what demographic you'll target, break down your list into a second column that measures your potential customer base. This customer base is what will make or break your project, and that is where you should focus most of your attention, your time and your resources. Make a third column for people you think might not like, or might not be attracted, to your ideal shop. At this point, you will decide to try to woo these consumers or decide if it's worth the energy to appeal to this limited segment of people. Who knows? They may surprise you by becoming your most loyal patrons. That is something you can only find out by trying it out.

I recommend that you observe anywhere from 3 – 6 locations at a time while you're pursuing a location. This will help assure a site agreement in a more timely fashion than if you do it one site at a time.

TIME OUT

Team Huddle

Selecting partners in business is no less serious than selecting life partners.

Two young men opened a coffee shop in a medium size mall. Four months later they went out of business.

One of the partners told me his colleague was never around to do any of the work. Obviously he thought raising the money via a family loan was his half of the partnership. The second partner was not prepared to work 14 to 16 hours days to build a success of which he only owned half.

Clearly they had failed to adequately discuss who would do what.

Two sisters opened a store together and throughout all my working with them, I had the feeling they were starting this business in the hopes it would bring them back together. Not unlike a couple having a baby and hoping it will save a bad marriage.

Well, six months later one sister was gone and the other and her husband were running the store and suing the sister who had left.

I have had the good fortune of having two outstanding partners. I would not have wanted to build our businesses alone. We succeeded because of the respect and trust for each other. More than that, we did some real serious soul searching before agreeing to be partners with each other. Then we discussed our ideas and expectations with an experienced financial management advisor to benefit from his objective perspective before proceeding.

If, in the planning stage of your business, you are uncomfortable to ask you future partner any question whatever, then you need to consider that just possibly you and this other person may not make good partners. Incidentally, look first at yourself to see if you think you are the nature of person who will be a good, considerate, thoughtful and dedicated partner.

Section III

Plan Your Work

Chapter Seven

Don't Even Think About It!

Expecting to file a Chapter Seven? Try not to be so negative. Proper preparation and study will help you to avoid the pain and sorrow of bankruptcy. Let's move along, shall we?

Chapter Eight

The Business Plan

Now, Why do I need this again?

A business without a plan is like a ship without a rudder

The next few pages outline steps for creating a business plan. In reality, any well thought out and well-written plan can be effective.

Writing a good plan is essential for success. It can be a frightening process putting on paper what has only been, up until this point, an idea in your head. Once you set aside your fear the process can be a validating experience.

Consider if you will, what would happen if you went to an airport and told the agent that you wanted to go on a trip, but you don't know where you are going, much less when you want to depart or arrive. How could the agent provide a ticket? A business plan is a similar scenario.

> A *Davidism:*
> Write a plan
> for yourself
> *that you*
> *believe in* and
> others can't
> help but
> believe in it,
> also.

Your plan is like your itinerary. It is a well-marked roadmap that will guide you to success. A business that is not based upon a written plan is like a ship without a rudder to steer it and no charted course to follow. How in the middle of a voyage will you have any confidence you could reach your intended destination?

So, why is it that business-people wouldn't write and follow a plan? Incidentally, now that you are thinking this deeply about business, that makes *you* a business-person. I've found that there are three common reasons, why someone so involved in commerce might not want to write a thorough business plan.

First, some think there is some secret, special way to write a business plan and they are also afraid of embarrassing themselves. I hope you don't believe this, because it's just not true. Whatever you feel is the best way to represent yourself and your interests will be the best plan for you.

Second, many think they are writing a plan in order to get money, so they assume that after the loan is approved, based on the plans content, that the plan has served its' purpose. This is completely incorrect. You should be writing a plan you can use to keep yourself focused and to measure your progress toward your objectives. This plan is for you, you are just allowing the bank or investor to view your business plan, making them confident that if you follow this plan you can and will pay back the loan.

Third, people are hesitant to actually create the numbers. Part of this is a fear of over-committing, while for some it is a fear of facing reality. Most of the time it is just plain, simple procrastination. Regardless, there is no reason at all to fear this part of the process.

You may not want to take the time to research and learn enough about the market and the business so that you're able to create realistic numbers. Maybe you're a shoot from the hip kind of person and feel that you can make anything succeed, with or without hard work and research. Okay, go for it, and good luck, but I must tell you, you will avoid many setbacks with a good financial plan (not the least of which is avoiding shooting yourself in the foot before your gun clears the holster).

Perhaps you're avoiding the numbers just because you don't know how to do it. Maybe word "estimate" sounds a lot like the word "guess"…and if you're just guessing at the numbers, why bother…because how can you ever convince someone else that you know what you're doing…particularly if you don't believe in the numbers you're writing down?

It is just this kind of over-anxiety and uncertain thinking that gets a loan turned down, or leaves a good idea unrealized. If you have these types of feelings, remember that the noun "estimate" is based on cold, hard facts, and the verb "estimate" is to make an informed opinion. And, the more informed the opinion is, the closer the estimate will be to actual fact.

You may even enjoy creating your business plan more if you get help from a professional in the field. This expert can aid you in developing projections and budgets that are not just guesses, but are realistic assessments, objectives, ideals and goals. If this option is attractive for you to afford and might prove to be unusually beneficial then visit **www.thecoffeecoach.net** and I can help refer you to experts.

Beginning a business plan is like planning a vacation itinerary. Steven Covey, the celebrated business writer, admonishes us to "Begin with the end in mind". Again, there are a lot of questions that you need to ask yourself to make the most pleasant and enjoyable trip possible.

- Who is embarking upon this voyage?
- Where are we going?
- Why are we going?
- How much will everything cost?
- How will we know when we have arrived?
- What's the best sort of craft to use? (As in the legal structure)
- What is this trip going to accomplish?
- What products and services are we going to purvey?
- Where should we locate?
- What days and hours will we be on the schedule?
- Where are our customers located?
- Who are your customers, and how many traveler's checks do they have?
- How will we be faster and stronger, avoid accidents and stay more healthy than the competition?

- What government departments have regulations that affect me? What are they?

We are moving into a section where you will need to get out your notes and those brainstorming memos to help you make a new, and cohesive beginning. This business plan will become a tool you can use to help explain your overall idea and may be essential in attracting the capital dollars you'll need.

Do what you can to make it as readable and accurate as possible. This is where you answer in writing the "Who, What Where, Why and How" questions we've addressed in the earlier sections. These are preliminary steps before even embarking on the comprehensive business plan.

When you begin to edit and refine your plan, think about the advice from Peter Drucker, another revered business writer: "So What and who cares?"

Step 1. Start by answering these specific questions, and any others you can think of that I haven't included. Feel free to use or copy this form or perhaps write one up for yourself.

Full Name: _____

Members of household: _____

Day Phone: _____

Evening Phone: _____

Home Address: _____

Work Address: _____

Other Address: _____

Am I ready to own my own business?   Y___N___?

Is coffee the business I want to start?   Y___N___?

Do I want to open with a bar___ a Kiosk, ___ or a store___?

Do I have the capital ($30,000-$90,000) to begin? Y___N___?

If no, how will I finance this business_____?

Do I have good credit_____?

Personal loans. From whom_____? How much_____?

        Who else_____? How much_____?

        Any others_____? How much_____?

Credit card credit. How much debt_____? How high is the limit_____?

Bank loans, how much? _____?

Bank name(s)_____? Interest Rate(s)_____?

Collateral_____?

Collateral_____?

Collateral_____?

Lease financing of equipment. Where_____?

Will I own and operate Y___ N___?

Will I own and hire others to operate Y___ N___?

How much money must I earn from this business in Year one _____?

                          Year two _____?

                          Year three_____?

How many hours a week can I work at this business_____?

What types of location will I seek_____?

Why should I get that site? _____?

What are my reasons for selecting this site?

_____

_____

_____

_____

E-mail this to **www.thecoffeecoach.net** for a consultation.

Step 2. Speak with the Health Department. After you've made the decision of what kind of specialty coffee business you want to open and generally where, you need to see the health department about food licensing requirements. You need to be familiar with these regulations to properly evaluate and negotiate for space. You will also need to generate a health department presentation in many situations.

Step 3. Survey several potential locations. You will need to have a list of location alternatives you can present to the Health Department. I *know* that there is probably one special place you've always wanted to house your business but, sometimes, your hopes and dreams may not match up to health codes. Planning out an alternative or two will provide the flexibility you will need to help you avoid spending money on changes that you may not be able to afford. It will also help you avoid delays in opening while you rush into code conformance.

Step 4. Begin a personal log -Write a personal letter to yourself explaining what you want to do, why you want to do it and when you feel would be the best time for implementation. Keep in mind that you're not writing this letter to share it with others. It's just for you. This will encourage you to be more honest about your dreams, fantasies, fears and hopes. This will be a terrific start. The next thing to include in your new log are the explanations of how much things will cost, how long things will take and what the results will be when success arrives. Every few weeks, update the letter and the log and review your previous entries. You'll be surprised at how much you can learn from looking back at your previous attempts before moving forward to try it again. Don't worry, sometimes the pursuit for financing will be an arduous, lengthy process, but that will leave you more time for ideas and for planning. List the things you've tried that have and have not worked. This exercise will help to keep this whole procedure in perspective.

Step 5. Address these three statements:

1. State those things *you know* about the industry.

2. State those you *think* or *guess* you know.

3. State those things you simply *do not know* and need to learn.

These steps will help you to know where to devote the most attention in the following planning section. Let us proceed.

Chapter Nine

How To Write A Business Plan

> Write your business plan the way you think and talk so that you will want to use it often.

A good business plan is an indication that you have taken your business idea through a strong process of examination, made certain you are clearly focused, have solid expectations, a methodical approach and good objective measurements along the way to assess your progress. That's an important sentence so read it again.

A good business plan is an indication that you have taken your business idea through a strong process of examination, made certain you are clearly focused, have solid expectations, a methodical approach and good objective measurements along the way to assess your progress.

A great business plan is something that has your personal touch in it. Here is my how-to list, top to bottom, 1-10, of what I've seen succeed for business plans, and would do again.

1. **Introduction**- what do you intend to be or to accomplish? What is the mission of this business? This is also something of a mission statement or a letter of intent. Also this might include a list of the key points that are specific to your business, or what sets you apart from many other competitors. No need to make it too extensive, this is after all the introduction. However a statement of what aspects will be covered within the plan or a table of contents is appropriate at this point.

2. **Your Store**- Where? Why here? What will be special inside to make customers love to return? This may have some anecdotes about the store set-up or the beginning of the idea, as well as some history of the location and biographies of key personnel. By the way, keep in mind what you hope to pay for overhead,

lease, utilities, product, and labor. Consider this now and include it in the financial projection section.

3. **Management**- who will work in the organization? Who will specifically be in charge of managing what? What skills, interests, experience and education does each of these people bring to the business that answer why will that task be done well? What outside management services will you employ? Who will you rely on as your outside advisor and/or mentor? Are there board members with a certain collective experience? All these considerations need to be covered in the Management section of your plan. Further management information will be covered in this text in the Nuts and Bolts section.

4. **Products and services**-What specific products and services will you offer? What are all of the costs involved in delivering the product and or service, as well as the delivery to you? How much must be sold to break even? What is your unique selling advantage, meaning, why will customers buy from you instead of the competition? Will there be opportunity to add other products or change your offerings in the future to elicit more revenue and profit?

5. **Marketing and analysis**-While you are welcome to use this book as source material, you will do well to conduct some local direct market research. You need not go more than a one or two mile radius for this. I have suggestions that make this relatively easy.

   i. Get to your local library and read reference manuals, industry specific books and recently published articles about the characteristics of the coffee market. More importantly, take a stroll in the neighborhood surrounding your prospective location. Observe who is there you can sell to or to compete with. Sit in a

68

coffee shop, notice people who might be approachable and chat with them, maybe even find some future customers. Just come right out and ask people what they want. Hand out surveys, go to the local hubs, take a day at the mall with a clipboard and offer some samples. This is the objective information needed to support what you believe about locations that you are seeking. Take some notes, and go ahead and analyze it, and put the results in your business plan.

ii. Ask local coffee house owners for an hour of time and be prepared to pay about $50 to $75 an hour for their ideas and advice. Remember to share this with your consultant so it can all be viewed and put in perspective.

Incidentally, this is another good time to differentiate yourself from your local competition, for yourself and for your proposal. What do you think is the best way to do it? How will competitors react to you entering the market? What is your pricing strategy? What's your plan for sales promotion and for later growth? What is the relative population of the market place in which you intend to operate? Which is more promising, walk-by or drive-by traffic? You actually may know by now, but include in the plan who will buy your products? Why will they buy from you, instead of your competitors? And how much will you actually sell? This might be the most comprehensive portion of your treatise, and it should be.

6. **Sample Menu**-This may be the most fun for you during the course of this project. It's specific, but it's enjoyable, and you're welcome again, to use any of the suggestions and ideas I've included in the 5th section, while definitely adding some of your own. Feel free also, to make up new names for your menu items that will lend to the ambiance of your store.

69

After your menu is clear and you have discussed the procedures you intend to follow for food preparation and so on, we are prepared to begin the equipment list. This will help refine your capital budget.

This process is also important so you can decide the equipment layout which will permit the designer to identify exactly where power, water, drains and so forth need to be placed.

7. **Financial Projections**- What is your total start-up expense? What might be the expenses you don't expect yet? What do you project will be your monthly operating costs? How much funding will you need to buy equipment and pay operating expenses for several months without taking money out of the business? You must expect that your revenue will start lower than you hope and might take several weeks or months to build up to your projected profit level. Where will you obtain the funds to begin this business? Project your sales, income and expenses for the first 12 months. Now create a plan assuming the lowest and highest projections. Some lenders prefer that you have three different financial scenarios. If you were a banker, would you loan money to this project? Good, since in addition to your private investors, you are primarily your own banker.

8. **Financial Requirements and Cash Flow**-What will you need to pay out each month and on which date? Include all of it: lease, product, utilities, travel, incidentals, labor, and construction.

9. **Calendar**- List the critical steps to beginning your business and the dates by when each step will be accomplished as well as by whom. Make short-term goals. Make long-term goals. Identify barriers and obstacles. What are the risks? What could go wrong? What interrupting effects might that have and how can

you prepare for them so that they don't delay the opening of your business? And, of course, plan for the holidays, local events, promotions, as well as other distractions that could stretch out your opening day. Every day of delay is a day of lost sales revenue.

Some times this part of the process can seem overwhelming. I have created a few simple tools to assist you in organizing the project so it is easy to plan every day and stay on schedule. Write me at **www.thecoffeecoach.net** for a back planning and business model on diskette.

10. **Other Info**-Include any thing else you might feel is necessary: appendixes, addendums, glossaries, and any materials you may wish to refer to in the future.

Now you can see how uncomplicated it can be to write a solid business plan and how well you are to prepared to write one. We also offer a sample menu planner at **www.thecoffeecoach.net** that you can order to work from.

Congratulations! You are ten steps ahead of most business-people in the entire United States of America. However, and not to diminish this creative spark of yours in the least, having created a thorough business plan is only part of this, your important undertaking. You will likely do a first draft of your business plan before contracting for a site. Adjustments to this business plan will be needed after you have selected a location, established your final menu, priced equipment, estimated traffic and the rest of the fun stuff.

More Important Questions:

- Do you now feel more comfortable writing the initial draft of your business plan?

- If you still have hesitations, visit **www.thecoffeecoach.net** and order the disk. The samples will be written in MS Word and the financial sheets will be prepared with MS Excel.

Chapter 10

All right I admit it. I sneaked

Select the approach that best fits your total situation

one over on you, but I wanted you to learn to do a business plan before anything else. However, before you start your business from scratch, we should discuss the alternative of buying someone else's business. Ask yourself why you should start from scratch if, for just a little effort, you might find a business you like that someone else would be willing to sell to you. You might get lucky, to find a place in an ideal location that is relatively easy for you to afford. But there are many considerations regarding the purchase of another's business.

- Does it already have an existing flow of customers? Was there mismanagement involved that you can avoid? Is the market over-saturated, is there a change in traffic patterns, is it just in the wrong area?

- Why is it for sale?

- The seller might already have experienced employees that you can choose to re-hire, or let them go.

- Work procedures, manuals, shifts, distributors, may already be established but seldom will they be well organized or even written down.

- This business might be doing just fine, but then again it may not. This is when you need your business plan experience, and the research you've already completed. Can you figure out why the seller is selling?

- Is this a business you really want to own? Seriously, will you be able to put forth the necessary effort involved? Is it a location that you'd wish for? What is your feeling about the location, what is your guess, what is your estimate? The key question is *why are you wishing to buy*?

- Exactly what is the customer flow, cash flow and net income? Do you trust the numbers you've been handed or should you do more research

- Do the liabilities of involvement with the former owner outweigh the benefits of the purchase?

- What do you need to invest to clean it up or remodel, repair equipment, or to increase shop appeal or improve drink quality?

- Where do you intend to get the money, or will the previous owner work out a simple pay out schedule?

- How do you determine what the company is worth? What is it worth to you? This might be a good time to have a talk with that expert you know. A business is worth just exactly what you are willing to pay for it.

- Would this business be more fun to own than starting my own project. Is it actually possible to eventually do both?

Buying or selling a business is most successful when both parties focus their attention on common goals, such as: to make a fair profit as soon as possible, to retain loyal, daily, paying customers, recruit new customers and to *always* keep in mind the needs of both parties to make an equitable exchange. Perhaps another thing to consider is if the seller is inclined to take on a limited partner, and if you could stand sharing the vision as well as the responsibilities and costs with someone else. This might be a good option for someone just starting out, but be absolutely sure to back yourself up with the advice of a competent lawyer and or accountant.

This is a good place in the book to discuss some other common approaches to starting a new business. You can start from scratch, buy a franchise or pay a license fee to use the brand, trademark recipes and so on of an established company. Each one can be the right solution depending upon the individual and the specific situation and goals of that person.

Buy – Build – Licence - Franchise

I have seen new coffee house owners successfully employ these distinct approaches to open a new business:

- Create from scratch and operate independently.
- Purchase the business from someone else.
- Operate under a license.
- Buy a franchise.

The potential for success is definitely there for all four approaches, but it should be pointed out that every one of these requires you to climb a mountain of details and work before the business you will own can be called a success. Far too many people enter this business unaware of the myriad of details that make up the recipe for success. Lets see how these approaches stack up.

- An *Independent Owner* is one who starts from scratch, does it all and builds her/his own place or business. You must create a concept, name, get licensed, research the market for a site, research suppliers, do your own negotiating, find a design and layout specialist, raise funds, supervise construction, buy and over see equipment installation, get trained, hire and train staff, publicize your business, pass inspections, receive inventory, clean and polish everything and market the heck out of your business.

Sounds like a lot of work doesn't it? Well it is, but by far the majority of coffee house owners have done just that. The result is that they are able to operate completely independently. They answer only to the business and their own integrity because they created their own thing and they are doing their own thing!

75

Part of the excitement comes from the creating and part from the independence and the rest from a sense of achievement all made sweeter by financial success.

- *When you buy*, you have the potential of gaining a lot of advantages. The business is already in place, customers are already coming in the door,, all you need to do is increase the speed and tweak the direction of the business, (if you are lucky). There are a lot of risks however. I won't go over the most obvious having to do with dishonesty and trickery or improper evaluation. No, the one I want to focus on is you and your dream:

Why are you interested in buying this particular place? Have you reviewed your self-examination and your business plan to make certain this fits into that category "Do my own thing"?

Please be careful to make sure you know why you want to do something. Just because you can is often the poorest reason to proceed. If it is "right" for you, it excites you, you can turn it into your dream, it is a place where you can make a difference, go for it.

- *Franchising*, especially in the food industry, is very popular. Why? Because opening any food business costs many thousands or millions of dollars. Over 75% of new independent restaurants fail in less than five years according to U.S. Department of Commerce data.

- Franchises often enjoy lower prices on goods due to price breaks for buying in mass for multiple units.

The coffee business, in our experience has a better than 85% success rate after five years. This higher success rate coupled with the lower cost of starting from scratch probably accounts for how few coffee franchises succeed. Almost all of the advantages, and there are many, generally available from a franchise can also be obtained from a licensed arrangement, so these will be discussed under the next heading.

Money is the biggest reason franchising has been only marginally successful. You must buy the franchise with an up front fee. The franchiser will require you to build out the store according to their specifications, which often is much higher cost than you may otherwise have spent. You pay a royalty percentage of all your receipts to the franchiser.

All of this can be the most intelligent investment for many especially if the franchiser really comes through with uniquely beneficial advertising, training, product quality and operating support.

One of the biggest problems with franchising is attitude and communication. A lawyer once convinced me not to franchise the Caffe Amore' concept with this statement, "Franchisees resent paying royalties forever because they seem to settle into one of two camps. When they succeed, it is not because you gave them the tools to do so, it is all because they work so hard and could have done it without you. When they are failing, it is not because they are poor managers, it is because your franchise is a poor one." One must ask, am I a potentially good franchisee? If yes, go for it!

- *Licensing* means you operate your own independent business but you have purchased the right to sell certain branded products of an established organization. There is no up front fee like in a franchise, and no franchise royalties.

The advantages of a franchise and license include:

- You take advantage of a road already traveled in a proven vehicle.
- The trademark, brand and logo are already established.
- Products, suppliers, and recipes are already successful.

77

- The operating procedures are already in place.
- Experienced experts help you select sites, employ designers, hire contractors, select and purchase equipment.
- You usually find their central purchasing is better priced than you can do on your own.
- Quality controls are already in place. Hiring procedures and training have been thought through & documented.
- The established theme and logo tie everything together. You can get into business faster and start with more momentum.

- The license will require you to buy certain products and equipment from the licenser or their approved vendors. You must abide by their recipes, names, and systems and permit periodic inspections.
- You sacrifice a little of your independence but not as much as under a franchise. Most licensing firms also offer regular monthly marketing programs for a nominal fee.

Whichever of these four you find is right for you, the same fundamentals are critical for success:

- ATTITUDE: A positive outlook
- PASSION: A love for the business
- PERSONALITY: Enjoy people and making them feel special
- WORK: A willingness to work hard
- LEADERSHIP: Be a good boss. Integrity, respect & honesty.
- QUALITY: Serve the best you can. Compete on quality not on price.
- LOCATION: You can make it or break it.
- LOGO: A distinctive theme and notable design.

- LOGO TEAM: A staff that cares to be the best
- MARKETING: Everyday and forever

Chapter Eleven

There is no Chapter 11 in this book.

As mentioned in Chapter Seven, let's try to maintain a positive outlook, shall we?

Chapter Twelve

<u>Build Your Own Place</u>

Done Well Is Done Once!

> # A professional design is not so much a cost as it is *an investment*

As I said earlier, the vast majority of clients want to do their own business from scratch, so let us proceed further into the building of your store.

How you design and lay out your coffee business will have a great deal to do with how much you enjoy being the owner for the next several years. Even if you are just opening a cart or kiosk, there are issues that may require the involvement of a professional designer because today most new carts are opening inside of buildings, not on the street or in a huge sports complex. Often, if one is buying a license or franchised concept, the seller will have a professional designer highly familiar with the coffee retail market available to help. Why so much emphasis on professional design? Can my friends and I do this by ourselves?

Yes, you can do it yourself, but if you are not a professional, it is likely you will make mistakes and result with a design that fails to afford you as much success as you deserve. Just as in golf or tennis, an inadequate backstroke results in an inadequate follow through; businesses that are started in an amateur manner usually produce an amateur result. When the big professional guys show up, the amateur approach often cannot compete effectively.

Design should first be focused on realizing your dream:

Consider first your own pride and enthusiasm. This is likely your first business. You will likely spend a lot of time working inside this space. You will be more likely to succeed if you are proud and enthused every day.

Second consider ease and comfort. Success demands that you have lots of repeat loyal customers. Customers will return more easily and often if you have designed around their ease and comfort.

Third, think about flow. Usually coffeehouses have brief periods of intense business activity. The more carefully one designs to achieve swift and smooth flow, the more money you can generate in these intense periods.

Next we need to showcase merchandise. Often lines of waiting customers will form. A design that showcases all your special merchandise will result in more impulse purchases, gifts for friends, a bag of beans for the weekend and so on.

Finally stores must be orderly and clean. There is no such thing as too clean in a coffeehouse. Dishwashers under the counter save labor time and remove dirty dishes from the customers' view. Professional back bar cabinets are an important consideration. Clean up sinks behind a wall are good if the space allows it.

Design also needs to be practical and pragmatic.

Is the design being driven by your vision? Do not allow your vision to get smothered. You are an independent business owner starting your first business. Do not allow yourself to accidentally end up running a store designed according to someone else's vision in place of yours. The design needs to be fitted to the space. This is the pragmatic element coming into play.

Focus on the flow. Can an entering customer quickly understand where to go to without needing to be told? What is the most convenient flow for the buy and go client without interfering with the sit

> A Davidism:
> A good
> design needs
> to consider
> color, tone
> and lighting
> coordination
>
> *Design it
> well,
> Build it
> ONCE!*

82

down clients? How can I position signs and merchandise so every customer can easily see all I have for sale?

Next, let's think in terms of new construction and remodeling.

If you will need to pull a building permit, prove you are complying with building codes and obtain inspection approvals along the way, you will be forced to have professional plans drawn that include an architect stamp.

If you will need to solicit competing bids, you will need professional plans to enable you to effectively compare the bids and select the best contractors. The drawings also afford you a basis to hold them accountable to perform according to the plans.

Incidentally, if you have no experience being a general contractor you may want the designers advice on how to hire one.

Everything needs to fit when the shop is finished and equipment is installed. Who is financially responsible to you to correct mistakes if they occur? With no plans to rely upon, it is likely that you will have no recourse to anyone.

Efficient equipment layout improves profitability.

Equipment and supplies should be positioned so I can serve the customer with minimal movement. There must be enough walking space so workers can move about without colliding.

We always try to prevent machine placement that requires operators to turn their back on the customer. If we can't avoid this, we like to mirror the back wall so eye contact can be maintained in the mirror.

Placement of the condiment stand should be done with forethought. Finally, and of extreme importance, let us discuss your signs.

People remember and notice things that are extraordinary. Signs should not be ordinary. People are frequently lazy. They read only a little bit or none at all so signs must be interesting if you wish them to be read. The reason most people use "specials" signs is that most people will read them. This way you can draw attention to another item every day.

When I started my first business, I did all my own research and design because I had a full time income and a lot of curiosity. Today I will definitely say that I would never start again without the professional guidance of a small business lawyer, small business accountant and an experienced designer.

TIME OUT

Team Huddle

Leopards do not change their spots. People that will cheat anyone, *will* cheat anyone, but more often end up cheating themselves. A man called one evening, three weeks after we installed a new espresso machine for him, reporting no heat in the boiler and no steam.

First thing next morning my associate and I arrived and found a cold machine with chocolate residue in the group heads, chocolate brown water in the site glass and the auto fill would not stop.

His employee showed us the chocolate mix and told us how the owner had shown her to use the espresso machine to make Mexican chocolate drinks that she and other employees had been doing daily since the machine had arrived (apparently he had not paid attention while being trained).

When the client arrived I asked if he had any idea what the problem was. He insisted the machine had been unplugged since the day we delivered it, as he was not yet open for business. He demanded we cover the repairs under warranty insisting we had delivered a faulty machine.

When we showed him the evidence and told him of the conversation with his employee he became angry and threatened to report our company to the Better Business Bureau and take us to court. We suggested he might wish to think about it and call us again. The next day, upon his request and approval we pulled the machine and spent more than 8 expensive hours removing hardened chocolate from inside the machine parts.

Obviously, the guy had tried to lie and steal the cost of repairs from us if he could. Often people who try to filch and cheat from their suppliers skimp and cheat on their customers. It is hard to change yourself.

This same man proceeded to buy coffee as cheap as he could and then skimped on the portions he used. He bought the sandwich bread and condiments for his store from a local warehouse grocery chain and tried to sell them as gourmet sandwiches.

The distinguishing clients you will appeal to will not be so easily fooled. His customer base shrank week after week until he finally closed the doors. He literally had cheated himself out of success because his original plan had demonstrated a really sound business idea and strategy.

Chapter Thirteen

Manage For Success

Be the kind of person people can trust

The first responsibility of management is to make a profit. Without profit, you cannot provide jobs, produce a benefit to others around you, deliver a satisfying product or service and it certainly is no fun. Now I am very hesitant in placing this strong of an emphasis upon profit, because while profit is essential, it is only the goal. It is not the primary purpose. To illustrate this distinction, I will again liken business to a sport such as golf. The purpose of golf is to have fun, enjoy the great outdoors, to spend time with family or friends, to strengthen relationships and so on. The goal of golf is to score low.

People who get these too confused almost always fail to enjoy the purpose and seldom score low. A business will fail to fill you with accomplishment and pride and also produce lesser profits if you lose your balance and fall too heavily on the side of make money, make money. Money can be such a miserable slave master!

The goal of business is to make a profit, but the purpose of your business must be something more important. My satisfaction, my purpose, is derived by my ability to encourage people and help them achieve a dream. For you it will be something distinct and unique to you.

Sometimes it is difficult for people to understand a phrase like "its' only money" Recently I saw Jack Welch, the retired head of GE, speak to a group of MBA students. He said something close to this, "*Life is* **profound**. *People, values and ideals are* **important**. *Business is just a game. Money is necessary to stay in the game, but don't permit yourself to take it so seriously that you forget what is important.*"

Money is essential. No business can prosper without profit, but hear me well. I have seen no one succeed who has allowed the goal of money to become more important than the goal of satisfying the customer with good service, quality products and a positive attitude.

I have also heard it said that Wall Street has a wise idiom. "Bears and bulls prosper where pigs get slaughtered". Greed kills!

That being said, I would add that the three most important *values* in business are Honesty, Integrity, and Balance. Maintain these qualities regardless of the profit margin, and you will be a more successful person, as well as likely to be a more successful business-person. Not only does practicing honesty and integrity keep you out of legal trouble, both these qualities engender great loyalty and trust. Whereas the books need to balance, taking a balanced approach to profit is important. Wishing and practicing and trying to score low in golf is pointless and woefully unsatisfying, if in doing so one destroys the pleasure and fun for your companions and yourself. Endeavor to maintain this tenuous balance, to excel at both the purpose and the goal.

You need to constantly measure the needs, progress and values during the course of running your business and this is accomplished by completing three types of reports:

A Profit and Loss Report, sometimes called an Income Statement, records your income minus your expenses for a given period of time. This report can be computed monthly, quarterly and annually. The "Bottom Line" of this report discloses the net income you earned or the net loss you experienced for that period of time. Often one needs to develop a projected Profit and Loss statement before commencing a business and again each subsequent year as part of your strategic planning and budgeting for the upcoming year.

A Cash Flow Projection is used to show when you will have cash in hand and when you need to pay bills. As your business grows, you may find that it is important to borrow money to finance expansion or growth. A cash flow projection will measure how much money you will need. Many times banks or others will ask for a 3-year cash flow projection. This is easy to do in some cases and absolutely impossible in many others. A generous dose of common sense will tell you if this is worthwhile in your situation.

I really do not think anyone can do a good job of creating more than a twelve-month cash flow projection before opening the doors. I would suggest you make a point of revisiting your start up cash flow after three or four months and revise it. This is likely to be more useful to you. It seems like a more common sense approach to me.

The Balance Sheet is a picture of the status or condition of your business at one point in time. Assets you own, such as cash, equipment, materials, inventory, patents, brand names, etc. appear in one column, usually the top or left. The liabilities, things you owe, plus your equity appears in the other column. It balances because *assets* are equal to liabilities plus equity, which includes paid in capital. Some people refer to equity as retained earnings.

Include this chapters' other ideas in a list of measurable assets and projections and let's do a quick review. Use your notes from earlier sections and form some concrete decisions. Do you know why and under what circumstances each of these following considerations will be useful to you? You might, at this point, return to that question, "What do I know?" and add some of the answers you are becoming more certain about.

- How do your qualifications and past experience prepare you to do what you need to do?

- Will you need employees, and approximately how many at any given time and circumstance?
- Where will you find them? Flyers, advertising in local papers, an employment agency?
- What will you be willing to pay, and what will you be able to pay?
- What specific skills do you need in your staff?
- Who will you rely upon for consulting, banking, legal and bookkeeping or accounting help?
- How can you make people aware of your company and their opportunity to purchase quality products here?
- Who will be responsible for what assignments?
- Who will co-manage with you, if anyone?
- Who will our suppliers be and what are the terms that will affect our relationship?
- What are the goals and objectives of this business 3, 5 or 10 years hence?

When you have re-read and revised your written business plan, you should be ready to decide the following:

- What types and amounts of financing do you need?
- What banking relationship do you want and where?
- What other partners or resources do you need to seek help from?
- When will your business open?

Well now you are pretty well prepared to read through the rest of this book and then start your own specialty coffee business. The creation of your business does not need to be overwhelming or frustrating if you utilize an orderly and methodical approach. Decide what you want to do and why you want to do it-and then *do it*. Create an action plan beginning from the opening date back to this week so you know what needs to be done each day and by whom. Measure your progress every day, in your personal log. The coach can assist you in creating a back plan if you wish.

This summarizes what we mean by the advice, *"Plan your work and work your plan."*

Chapter Fourteen

Managing Employees

Hire Attitude, Train For Technique

> ### *Al'ism:* Do it nice or do it twice
> (Al is a protégé of mine)

One major challenge involved in developing a solid business is hiring, training and retaining quality people. Consider the level of service you encounter in some fast food or other retail establishments.

Obviously management is not consciously encouraging poor service. Competition certainly demands you supply the best service possible and the competition for good employees is constantly increasing.

You must therefore conclude that it *is increasingly important to locate, develop and retain good employees.* Perhaps the most significant issues affecting your success with employees are:

- Your attitude
- Your expectations
- Your actions

The skilled artist behind an espresso machine is a "Barista". The accomplished Barista is an expert not only about espresso, but also specialty coffee, the equipment, customer service and showmanship. Personality, pride and a desire to serve exceptionally well are the difference between a fast food clerk and a barista with that special, professional touch.

Hiring

1. Prepare yourself for a structured interview.

    a. Write a simple job description, not more than 2 or 3 sentences.

b. Prepare a list of the important skills, abilities, experiences and attitudes for the job you have. How important is each: L-low, M- medium or H-high?

c. Prepare a list of open ended questions that will help you determine from each applicant the level they represent for each important feature you seek.

2. Use this approach for each applicant and force yourself to be consistent. Require others to use this same form when interviewing applicants for you.

3. Give each new employee a clearly written job description. Be very candid about your expectations

4. Provide a list of requirements and specific procedures to be followed.

5. Always check references.

6. Invest several days of organized training for each new employee. Make certain the employee knows where to find everything, how to make each drink, how to operate the cash register, including correcting errors and how to operate, clean and maintain all equipment. Order extra copies of the espresso standards, recipes and trouble-shooting guide to give to each new employee. You can order these from **www.thecoffeecoach.net**.

7. Have clear standards and *do not compromise these standards.* Selecting people is always difficult. We have found you cannot generalize; young, old, middle age, male or female. We've seen them all succeed. We have also seen them fail.

Keys to look and listen for include:

- Attitude. Lots of positive energy.
- Great eye contact.
- Enjoy working with varied people.

> Employees *do not* think like owners. That, in and of itself, is a good thing or else *they'd be owners*; perhaps even competitors.

- High professional standards but with a fun relaxed upbeat exterior.
- Clean. Particular about personal hygiene.
- A lot of smiles. I mean a lot!
- Extroverts-showmanship.
- Respects details, standards and procedures.
- Respects coworkers and customers.

The Barista's job includes many variables and tasks:

- Make consistently excellent espresso drinks.
- Pleasantly welcome every individual to try your products.
- Provide customers a fun and entertaining experience-*everyday.*
- Keep everything fresh, clean and orderly. Spotless is good.
- Know a lot about coffee and positively share this with customers.
- Give every customer excellent service-*everyday.*
- Pro-actively sell your service and products, especially the up-sell.
- Respect equipment enough to learn how to use it best, clean and maintain it, diagnose and fix most common failures.
- Able to serve many customers at high speed and remain enthused and pleasant.
- Experience in retail merchandising would be valuable in most stores and shops.
- Bartender or wait staff experience is often a good start for a cart or coffee house position.

When interviewing:

- Make the atmosphere comfortable.
- Listen carefully.

- Maintain eye contact.
- End the interview with clear communications about follow-up.
- Take notes.

1. Be realistic. Most employees won't think like you do. If they did, they would be your partner or your competitor.
2. Expect to have to constantly repeat and role model each of the principles you feel are critical to your business success.
3. Think through how an employee will hear you before you speak. Be clear. Mean what you say. Say it in a way that makes it easy for this employee to understand and <u>want</u> to achieve your desired outcome.

An example will help demonstrate these points. No matter how often you tell employees to never serve an imperfect drink, almost no employee will ever throw out a shot of imperfect espresso until they have seen one of the owners do so repeatedly. It is unlikely anyone ever showed them it is better business to discard imperfection than to serve a poor drink. Employees, as good as they can be, generally are reluctant to think and act like an owner, no matter how earnestly you coach them.

Constantly remind your employees that the customers are their audience and their *first priority*. Owners and managers are not always around to tell employees what to do or how to do it. Employees must be trained, "*Your job is to do whatever you can to give each customer an excellent experience at our bar.*" Management's job is to supply the tools, training, equipment and support needed by the employee to get that single job done better than the competition does it. The owners must serve their employees excellently and remove obstacles to good service at every opportunity.

This is hard stuff. It means keeping equipment in excellent order, providing repeat training, developing effective marketing approaches, demanding excellence of all suppliers and managing the business profitably so everyone has job security. Realizing you have a duty to your employees to keep them enthusiastic creates an environment where they will proactively sell your products and services without realizing they are.

Recognition-

Recognition is an important motivational tool. Often recognition can be more effective than money. Stay alert to opportunities to reinforce positive behavior and to reward positive performance.

- Visit employees at work just to say hello and thank them for doing a good job.
- Look for opportunities to say something positive each time you see an employee.
- Learn to use the word "*appreciate*" often. It's easy and it means so much when it's sincere.
- Be honest and clear. Integrity with self, employees, customers and suppliers will build a solid business foundation of respect.
- Respect others differences and alternative approaches. This way you don't have to solve every problem.
- Use *Certificates of Achievement*. These are available at any office equipment supply house.
- Plaques are a little more costly but can be very effective if used sparingly.

Pay for performance-

The state labor department usually can provide you with a wage survey of your area that will help you determine a competitive wage. Provide health benefits for employees who work beyond the probationary period. It also is likely your local restaurant association has examples and similar data.

Try to create a profit sharing pool equal to some percentage of the gross profit. This pool is distributed to all employees who have succeeded in exceeding their probationary period. The pool is distributed twice yearly based upon the ratio of hours worked. Establish practical goals to determine the payout of this bonus. The more you pay in bonus, the better your business.

You may arrange a health plan designed to prevent major financial difficulty for employees, but limits the monthly cost to your new business. A $500 deductible 80/20 plan is a good beginning. The company pays half the cost for covering employees who work over 25 hours a week. Employees who have completed 90 days probationary period and who do not have access to other group coverage are eligible.

Discipline

Communicate your job standards and hold everyone accountable everyday. Keep your procedures simple. Clearly define grounds for suspension or termination. When an employee violates one of these requirements, create a written record of the reprimand. Ask the employee to sign it and give them a copy.

Try very hard to avoid terminating anyone. It is not good business. If the job isn't working for the employee, we give them all the support we can to find work elsewhere. Life is just too short to spend any of it creating or harboring hard feelings.

Interview Questions

1. Why did you decide to apply for a job at _____? (Pay attention to their attitude. Is this just another job or are they interested in the Company, or the products we sell) what do you expect to find at _____ that you don't have at your present job?

2. How would you describe good customer service? Tell me about your own good shopping experience. Give me an example of a time you felt you gave more than required on the job/school? Were you recognized? How did you feel?

3. How would you describe yourself? (Get 3-4 descriptive adjectives)

4. Tell me about the best teacher or supervisor you have had and what made them the best in your mind?

5. What skills, talents, and experience do you have that you believe you could use at _____?

6. Describe the reasons you have missed scheduled work or school in the last year?

7. Can you give me an example of a way you have made your job/school assignment easier and/or more rewarding?

8. What would you do if you were asked to do something you were uncomfortable doing? (This question is vague for a reason, see if they respond to what they think you are asking or ask for clarification) ethics? Training?

9. What do you like least/most about your current job/school?

10. What gives you the greatest sense of accomplishment in your job/school?

11. How are you most comfortable getting a person interested in and willing to buy what you are selling?

12. Tell me about a time you went out of your way to help or provide service to a customer?

13. What can "you" do to get a customer to come back again?

14. How long were you at your last job before you felt comfortable?

15. How would you handle a situation were a customer or co-worker was very upset with you?

16. What would you do if you were quite sure a co-worker, that you liked and had worked with for a while was stealing?

17. What would a previous employer say if we were to call for a reference?

18. How would you handle a problem or conflict with a co-worker or supervisor on the job?

19. Over all appearance: (please use 3 descriptive adjectives)

This interview is designed to help you identify and measure the following dimensions:

- Work Standards- set high goals or standards for self, others, organization. Dissatisfied with average performance.

- Initiative - Active attempt to influence events to achieve goals, self starting, takes action to achieve goals beyond what is called for.

- Customer Service - Degree of personal need to help, satisfy, accommodate a customer. Sell and meet sales goals.

- Integrity - Maintaining social, ethical and organizational norms in job related activities.

- Motivation- the extent to which activities and responsibilities available in the job overlap with activities and responsibilities that result in personal satisfaction.

The present day finds us all in a very tight employment market. Owners are thus working more hours while they scramble to find help. The quality of staff is often less than in the recent past. So you are rushed and exhausted. If you train this new employee just like you did in the past, you probably won't like the result. Slow down, be more specific and precise because this employee takes more effort... Employees have lots of choices today so, more than ever before, it is the employer who creates an environment employees want to be in who will succeed. It is good to keep in mind the following Al'ism:

```
Al' ism:
Your staff
will do what
you inspect
not what you
expect!
```

TRAINING AND DEVELOPMENT

Whatever you invest in your store, equipment, products and so on, it is your employees and how well you develop them that will make the difference between you and your competition.

Under-training of employees is the second biggest error we witness in the market place daily. Consider this: you open your new store so getting trained is exciting for everyone. Later, you get so busy, you teach a lead person to train new hires. Then one day, that person trains another to do so. Then one day, an employee leaves unexpectedly so you need to temporarily fill the hours. You discover much to your surprise numerous procedures and drink techniques are different than you thought them to be. Suddenly you realize that many of the exacting quality standards you advocate have been lost over time. This is the all to often repeated pathway to mediocre quality and mediocre business performance that you need to avoid. This requires some organized preparation.

First, you need to attend to your own training, so you are competent to train others. Second, you need to be clear about job descriptions so you can focus your training on those things you expect this employee to be responsible for. Third, you need to acquire tools that will help you be consistent and thorough. Consistent quality requires consistent training.

The Coffee House Resource Manual that is available from the web site, is intended to be an operating guide similar to what one would obtain when purchasing a franchise. It contains in greater detail:

A Barista training guide

Suggestions on coaching and developing employees

Sample policies and procedures

People accept leadership from people in whom they have confidence. This means you must do all you can to learn the culture of specialty coffee before you can pass it along to others. This is a continuing process but here are some specific suggestions:

- Join the SCAA. Look over educational resources in it's Resource Center at SCAA.org and begin reading books about coffee and the specialty coffee world.

- Subscribe to premier industry trade publications.

- Attend the annual SCAA convention or NASCORE convention.

- Solicit educational material from the roasters you will be purchasing from.

- Choose an equipment supplier with proven education and training not only on machines, but barista training, preventative maintenance, effective marketing and more.

Now lets us shift to training employees.

All employees function better when they clearly understand what their job is and how you expect it to be performed. People need to understand the boundaries along with the opportunities. It also is good to remember that recognition and reward work better than rules and discipline if you are trying to motivate folks.

One of the better ways is to dedicate yourself toward giving employees clear job descriptions, first class repetitive training and the right equipment properly maintained. Again, the content of the Resource Manual is much more detailed, but here again are some suggestions:

The best training video I have used in the last 30 years is entitled **ESPRESSO 101,** produced by *Bellissimo*. It accomplishes its objectives better than any video I have ever viewed. I have viewed this film more than 30 times, and it always reminds me of something I have been under emphasizing.

The Barista Training Guide, available stand alone or integrated into the Resource Manual, will give you an excellent consistent training format to follow.

Ask your cash register supplier to provide specific training in money handling procedures.

Choose an equipment supplier with professional staff available to train your baristas in machine operations, drink making, customer service & more.

Work with a roaster who offers coffee classes, will host a cupping in their place as well as yours and who eagerly offers to repetitively educate your team.

Learn to coach individuals rather than boss them.

103

Training employees is not exactly the same as developing them. Let me quote from the Resource Manual: *"Leaders understand one does not manage employees, one manages tasks. People need to be lead and developed."*

Teach employees how you want customers treated. Ken Blanchard, a noted business management author suggests. "Look for opportunities to catch people doing something right and then compliment them in public. Always critique employees in private."

Customer relations cannot be taken for granted. You too, must teach this. The employee will believe more what you do than what you say. Often how you treat employees is how they will treat your customers.

Give all employees the same basic policies and procedures to live by. Avoid making exceptions as much as possible as that demonstrates that there really isn't a policy or procedure that must be followed. Give employees opportunity to have ownership of your mission and purpose. Treat employees as your most valuable asset so they learn how to treat your paying customers. Encourage thorough communication. Require all standards to be met all the time and make sure employees see you walk your talk.

Customer Service means so many different things to so many people that it is difficult to attempt to discuss the subject in depth here. Suffice it to say every customer should feel like a special honored guest in your home every time they visit.

Volumes have been written about customer service. A visit to your local library will perhaps be enlightening.

Chapter Fifteen

Profitability is your management's first responsibility

Is Your Idea Financially Realistic

Wake up and ...smell the money!

Who are the consumers of Gourmet and Specialty Coffee? Research from the Small Business Development Center says:

Most gourmet coffee drinkers live in large urban communities. Persons with some college education consume 11% above average, college graduates drink 49% above average, and postgraduates are an amazing 71% above average in specialty coffee consumption.

Most specialty coffee consumers are affluent, earning incomes of $35,000 and above. Those above $50,000 are 64% above average in Gourmet coffee purchases. Women purchase over 60% of all specialty coffee. Dual-income-no-children (DINC) households are particularly high consumers at 45% above the national average; working parent households are 29% above and single mothers 10% above the average. Espresso, first measured in 1989, represented 1% of the coffee consumed in this country. Consider the potential. In Italy, a nation less than 1/4 our size, there are over 150,000 espresso bars. More than 15 times that of the U.S.! (*Entrepreneur magazine*)

After analyzing this research you might conclude that you'd like to secure a site with a concentration of highly educated urban consumers with the disposable income to spend on fine coffee and who appreciate treating themselves to a luxury that costs less than $3.00 per cup.

While there still remains an ever-growing environment in large cities for profitable espresso bars, the past four to seven years (since 1995) we have seen widespread acceptance of coffee in smaller communities. Towns, as small as 1200, are now supporting active, profitable shops. The more successful bars there are, the more

105

room there is for new ones to open. 2002 and beyond will demonstrate to us greater acceptance of drive-up venues and that coffee will be added to every type of existing high traffic business you can think of: home improvement centers, child care centers, grocers, flower shops, and on and on and on. Combination shops are cropping up everywhere.

A shift has been occurring in the market for several years now and its momentum is increasing. Let us call it diversification. Coffee carts, due to limited space, continue to develop most of their revenue from drinks (coffee, espresso, granita and Italian sodas). Operators are however learning how to sell purified water, fresh juices and juice bar health drinks. Coffee houses rarely open without a sandwich and soup menu today.

Potential Profitability

You're asking yourself, *"How much money can I make in this business"* and the answer is, *"I don't know!"* Each owner and site is unique. I've reviewed the financial performance furnished by many equipment vendors in Seattle, Minneapolis, Atlanta, Chicago, Austin, Portland and other major metropolitan coffee markets. I am unable to find any *one thing*, aside from good coffee, that specialty coffee shops in these markets have in common. I have read with interest the news reports of how lucrative this business is and examined the financial results

> *A Davidism:*
> "Success is 10% inspiration, 30% preparation and 60% perspiration"

of my own business. I'm still unable to find any *one thing* that I've done that has contributed to our success. I *have* found, as you might expect, some pretty wild claims. This is a fascinating and profitable industry but it is *not* a get-rich-quick scheme, let me tell you. Hard work, good service, superior product and ideal location are as important to your success as it has ever been. Here comes another one of those philosophy nuggets. *"Success is 10% inspiration, 30% preparation and 60% perspiration"*

This is a good business and now seems the right time to get involved, but if someone has been filling your head with dreams of six figure incomes, you will be very disappointed. Yes, there are a few of those, but most owners are making much less from one location.

I encourage new operators to begin with a very conservative outlook. Assume you will begin with between 75 and 100 customers per day. Assume the average sale per transaction is $2.25. For the sake of argument lets place the number at 100. That's only $225.00/day. Yikes. Now, assume your total cost of goods sold is approximately 35% to 40%. That takes away $78.75 to $90.00. Labor, including your management wage, is usually 30% taking away $67.50. Add in a rudimentary marketing plan and your overhead consumes another 4% at $9.00. Okay, after your first day of business you have made $69.75. Now pay the rent and what is left? Seems pretty small, doesn't it? Well, times that by five, six or seven and then again by fifty-two weeks and you'll know how close you come to a profit. None too shabby for your first month, eh?

Now, go back and assume the average sales transaction is $3.25 and you'll immediately discover how important that particular number, and its supporting research, is to you.

Also assume your business requires constant attention for the first six months to increase your business by 50% to 100%. If you do better than this, you should be excited. If you do not, you should not be discouraged. Remember, this is not a get-rich-quick scheme. This business will grow as continuously and steadily as you demonstrate to your customers they can rely on you for quality products and extraordinary service at a fair price. Once you accumulate these loyal customers, they are far less likely to be won over by a competitor.

Potential new owners (often referred to as "wannabes"), are frequently subjected to stories of unfair experiences by their friends and family when the mention of starting a new business pops up. The most challenging three include:

First, lots of people who know nothing about the business have all kinds of good ideas of what you should do and how you should do it. Often these ideas are hard to resist and even harder to put into proper perspective. While these people may know nothing about the coffee business their loudly expressed ideas often sound authoritative. Don't be misled.

Second there are those who try to extinguish the fire of your enthusiastic new idea. "Are you sure? Don't you have a good job? Why on earth would you want to do that? Do you really think people in this town will pay those kinds of prices?" And on and on it goes. *Those who never try cannot succeed.* If people had taken this approach to your interest in bicycles, skates, swimming, skiing or any other of a hundred things, look what your life would have missed.

Third is that unanswerable, and I might say totally disrespectful, question, "Well, how much money do you think you can make anyway?"

When you have finished your business plan, you will be perfectly prepared to answer with confidence, " I know precisely how many customers I need daily to break even so I won't go broke. I also know how many more I need so I won't be tempted to quit and go back to working for someone else. Finally I know how many I need to also produce an acceptable return on the money I am investing."

When you know these answers, you will have more power over your business future than almost anyone you know.

Potential Costs

Coffee should be purchased only from a specialty coffee roaster. The quality of your product begins with the quality of the coffee you put into the "group head," (the espresso brewing device) before pressing the brew control button. The best coffee available costs about $6.50 to $10.00 per pound. I am highly suspect of coffee available at below $5.50 per pound wholesale. Premium grade arabica coffee cannot be priced this low. Cheap coffee pretending to be top grade can be purchased for this and even less, but it is in itself a lie.

You may also hear claims by different espresso machine retailers that you can sell more cups per pound with this or that machine. You should definitely discount these claims. Ask your coffee roaster how many cups per pound you should expect to sell. The math isn't all that difficult and you'll be able to base much of your information from a knowledgeable source.

Generally speaking, you will sell 55 to 60 shots of espresso per pound. Attempting to produce more than that per pound will damage the quality of your product and spell the beginning of the end for your business. You should see that one pound of coffee should produce between $80 and $150 gross revenue with some allowance for waste. Why risk your business reputation for the few additional pennies profit difference using cheap coffee? Buy great coffee and deliver top quality products and your public will be content to pay you a fair price.

Consider, at 60 cups per pound, if I save $1 per pound it means less than $.02 per cup. The business is wiser to buy quality coffee for $1 more and raise prices $.05 per cup. Buying cheaper coffee, in this example is only stealing profit from yourself. Some would call this "snatching failure from the jaws of success". Remember, price is a strategy, not an emotional reaction. You do not really think customers will stop buying from a store with a friendly atmosphere, great service and consistent quality for a nickel a cup, do you?

The cost of paper products will vary widely ($.04 to $.07) between plain generic versus custom printed items. Customized cups can be a very valuable marketing investment, however, the volumes needed to achieve discounted pricing may exceed the needs of a single site operator. Similarly, the cost of personalized napkins or private labeled coffee may be out of reach for many operators.

Many coffee suppliers offer cups with their logo. Some will even have porcelain or china cups available to their customers.

When accepting logo cups from your roaster, you will be able to order in convenient volume, and you will definitely gain from the professional appearance of their design. You are, however, building their image not yours with each sale.

Cups are even available with varying methods of insulation so the customer doesn't burn their hand. This eliminates the need for double cupping or additional insulating sleeve like devices. This type of cup costs a little more than straight paper and is a point of consideration when you are watching you overhead costs.

We switched years ago to the highly compressed recyclable foam cups. They are more earth friendly than plastic lined paper cups, provide better insulation, avoid the cost of double cupping or insulating sleeves, and there are no taste modifications.

Food items purchased from a wholesaler and sold at <u>cart/bars</u> generally cost 50% of their sale price. Most food is carried and sold as a convenience to your drink customer, as well as a collateral draw, depending on the quality of the food. It is the drinks that carry the high profit margin, and must always be your staple.

<u>Coffee houses</u>, by contrast, with the ability to prepare their own sandwiches, soups and bake cookies, muffins, etc. will discover they can lower food costs to about 30% to 35% and dramatically increase profits.

Your gourmet coffee costs should be around $.08 to $.12 per 8oz. prepared serving and you'll be selling it for between $.95 and $1.55 per cup. A Latte may cost you $.28 and sell for $1.65 to $3.00. Flavored lattes may bring as much as $4.00 at many coffee shops. Add a second or third shot of espresso and sell it for .75c per shot. Add flavoring and sell it for $.25 to $.45. The potential for successful profitability is, within reason, endless.

Most people, selling between $150 and $250 per day will realize 55% to 65% of their gross sales before taking their labor deductions. When your daily revenue goes above $300, the margins improve markedly. When you own and operate the bar, it is fairly simple to estimate the potential pre-tax income.

It is common, in stores doing over 300 daily transactions, for the cost of merchandise, coffee, cups, sugar, flavorings, condiments, etc. to reduce to a range of between 20% and 25% of gross sales.

Up selling is the art of enticing customers to buy more than the single drink they order. "Would you like a double?" or "Would you like a shot of hazelnut in that" or "May I add a topping of whipped cream?" are signs of an experienced barista. This up-selling skill is often the difference between an adequate versus highly profitable operator.

Financial Performance

Please keep in mind that the financial projections included in this book are only examples. There is no conceivable way that these numbers can accurately predict the way your specific business will perform. Always take the time to create number estimates upon facts that you have spent the time researching. Be sure to review these with your accountant and/or lawyer, and compare them to the research and estimates you already have. Review the following examples and develop your own set of assumptions to best fit the business you are planning:

Example 1: You are the owner of a six-day a week operation. Let's assume that you open for business 8 hours a day, adding an hour before and after for opening and closing procedures. Let's figure you'll serve up to 200 customers daily. You should plan on adding an employee for four hours everyday when the two of you start doing 200 to 300 cups a day. Then you might increase your additional part-time labor to eight hours after three hundred cups. Rent is estimated at $1,000 monthly.

Income projections assume your customers do the following:

- 40% drink specialty drinks, 60% drink coffee.
- 15% buy pastry, 20% buy a soup or sandwich and 7% to 8% buy juices, water, candy etc.
- We assumed a bank loan of $55,000 at 10% paid over 5 years

You can create another pro forma using many of the factors above but following the outline in Example 2 below.

Example 2: A seven-day operation. You are an investor-owner, not an owner-operator. An employee manager works eight hours each day, up to 150 cups per day, adding a second 4 hour helper between 150 and 200 cups, and then a full second 8 hour person when demand exceeds 200 cups.

Example 3: A seven-day retail operation where you open 1.5 hours before the mall does to serve the arriving employees. You remain open until the mall closes. You, the owner, are assumed to work the first two hours each day and six hours during the late afternoon and early evening high traffic hours. Rent is computed at $15 per foot plus $5.50 for "Triple net".

Triple Net is a term commonly used in commercial space leasing. It means your share of the cost of taxes, insurance and common area maintenance is added over and above the rent paid for the space you actually occupy.

Example 4: You are the owner of a coffeehouse or deli. Your main business is lunch sandwiches and a food delivery service to local businesses. You have 2 employees. Your rent is $750 a month for 1000 sq. feet.

The Integrity Of Your Roaster Is Very Important

Green coffee costs rise and fall like any other agricultural product. The worst seems to be over and prices have settled back a little from the high point. It is unlikely green coffee prices for premium grade Arabica will ever fall below $1.00 a pound again, but higher prices for the grower are a good thing for all of us. The prices we pay for coffee must make it affordable and profitable for growers or they will cease growing the crop we need for our business.

One reason to be careful to select a roaster of the highest integrity is the ease with which unscrupulous sellers can cleverly mislead people like you and me. Many of us are concerned about buying coffee that is organically grown, shade grown and supports sustainable agriculture.

These are all terms many people use misleadingly or outright dishonestly. Some plantations with as little as one shade tree on an entire acre will advertise their coffee as shade grown. Some roasters will claim to offer organic coffee without actually meeting the certification standards required to grow organically.

If these are important issues to you, the professionals in our network and also the Specialty Coffee Association of America can lead you to experts in the industry who can help protect you from fraud or deception.

NOTE: Store operating procedures and schedules for opening and closing are addressed in The Coffee Academy's *Operation Manual*. The Coffee Academy has also created a detailed *Barista Training Manual*. Both are available from:

www.thecoffeecoach.net.

Chapter Sixteen

Be orderly so that you can avoid a crisis during your most inconvenient times.

Financing

How do you get a space and enough equipment? Easy. You have about three options:

- Buy with Cash
- Borrow from a bank or family members
- Lease

Okay, maybe not so easy, but here's some information to help you better focus your energy.

When borrowing through a banker, the lender usually requires the buyer to make a significant down- payment. Often the lender also will require other collateral pledged as security for the loan.

When you purchase an asset for cash, you are spending today's dollars rather than cheaper dollars two and three years forward-inflation reduces the future dollar. You usually need to account for the asset on your balance sheet. You *are* permitted to depreciate the cost of the asset over 5 to 7 years as an offset to taxable income.

When you lease equipment, you are actually financing the purchase over several years.

Cash

Machines are usually purchased for cash or leased, but some rental options exist. The lowest direct cost, of course, is to purchase for cash. It is common to pay all cash up front with a small discount earned for this prepayment, or to pay 50% down and the other 50% on the day of delivery.

Borrow

It usually is cheaper for you to borrow money from your bank, credit union or life insurance than to make lease payments or rental payments to a dealer. However, tax issues for some individuals makes leasing attractive. Bank loans may cost from 10% to 15%, however most banks will be unwilling to finance your entire purchase.

Another limitation of banks is that you do not want to consume all of your available credit. It may be wise to lease some or all of your equipment and rely on the bank for other areas of financial support. This leaves your business with a little flexibility in the event additional capital is needed later. Keep in mind that more businesses fail from a lack of operating capital than for any other reason.

It often is easy to increase your credit card limit and purchase equipment with a credit card. This may carry a slightly higher interest rate than your bank, but will be substantially easier than other options. Also, you have freedom to pay off the entire balance anytime you wish.

Leasing

Is it better to lease equipment or borrow more from the bank and pay cash? The answer depends upon each individual's specific situation, their preferences as to cash management and their tax situation but we can provide some objective information to help you become a little more informed about the differences and basis for making this choice.

The entire cost of the equipment can be covered in a lease. Leases allow you to take the full monthly payment as a tax-deductible expense; thus you depreciate the asset in 3 years typically instead of five to seven. You recover the investment faster.

Leases are not considered long term debt, so they do not appear on your balance sheets. Your business looks better to other lenders. Most leasing firms allow you to add equipment or upgrade equipment during or at the end of a lease with no additional qualifying paperwork.

Perhaps most importantly, leasing allows you to keep hold of more of your investment capital as a reserve. Most small businesses fail due to lack of adequate capital and this is a handy way to safeguard yourself.

Sometimes equipment outlets and retail spaces will take a portion of the total costs to help you get started. However, you must know that you will pay much more for these agreements in the long run than some other methods. But if that's the only way for you to get started, then it might be the best option for you.

Other Considerations

Leasing is a good safeguard for equipment that is changing rapidly due to technology advances, like computers and copiers or many "super automatic" espresso machines. The computer system you paid $4,000 for two years ago can be replaced today with new and more advanced capability and software for half or less. Leasing may have been wiser than buying.

Leases have variable end of lease options; Fair market value, $1 buy out & 10% purchase option. Each of these indicates a different way you can own the equipment after completing the schedule of monthly payments. Fair Market Value offers the lowest monthly payment and highest cost to purchase at the end of the lease. The $1 option means you can buy the equipment for $1 after having paid the full schedule of payments. The monthly rate is a little higher than a Fair Market lease. The 10% option has a lower monthly payment than the $1. One payment of 10% of the original equipment value paid at lease end and you own the equipment, or you can upgrade equipment and keep making monthly payments. Personally, I prefer the 10% purchase option.

Lease Qualifications

Any existing business with a good credit history and more than two years operating track record can usually qualify for a lease. Just complete an application, give two or three references and have a sensible average bank balance and you are good to go. It can be somewhat more challenging to get new owners qualified for a lease, but the better quality and professional machine suppliers can often achieve this for you when others cannot.

Completing a lease application, by the way, does not obligate you to anything. It is like going to a lender to pre-qualify for a home loan. You will need a "clean" personal credit history. This means no bankruptcy, court judgments, or collection problems with things like credit cards, school loans and so on.

Let's look at an overview to put things into perspective, and to determine how ready you are to proceed and to apply for funding

- First consult with several coffee business owners to gain an idea of those things you will enjoy or not about this business.
- Call the secretary of state and register as a business. They will give you a tax I.D. number. Take that number to a bank and open a commercial bank account in the name of your business with $5,000 or more. Do not spend one nickel of this money until all of your financing has been projected and determined.
- Find an espresso equipment supplier with an outstanding reputation for helping people succeed from scratch.
- Complete your straightforward and preliminary Business Plan and secure the best location.
- Develop a comprehensive budget of start-up capital.
- Prepare a personal financial statement and gather your tax returns for the past 3 years.

- Call the credit bureaus, TRANS UNION, EQUIFAX or EXPERIAN to get a copy of your credit report and clear up any errors (1-888-567-8688).
- Arrange all your financing. It is often wise to decide to buy things that appreciate and lease things that depreciate.
- Finalize the <u>profit and loss,</u> <u>cash flow</u> and <u>asset</u> statements
- Prepare a back planning action chart to get you from this stage to the first day your business will be open.

Okay, being this prepared means you are ready to arrange your financing.

Forming a legal company.

First you need to form a legal entity for your business. This may be a sole proprietorship, a corporation, and a partnership or in some states a Limited Liability Company. If you have never done something like this before, do not panic. This is not difficult and there are many sources of help.

- You might talk to a small business lawyer and your accountant. The lawyer can do all the legal papers for you.
- You might want to visit SCORE or your Small Business Development Center first. Both of these organizations will give you free advice and will have the phone numbers and addresses you need for both state and federal registration.
- A call to your state Secretary of State or Secretary of Commerce will also be helpful.

When you have decided upon the legal structure of the company you will own, you must register that name with the federal and state governments. They will in turn supply you with a tax identification number. You do not exist as a business without this Tax ID number.

118

Banking

When you have your tax identification you can go to your bank and create your business account.

We suggest you force yourself to pay all bills and invoices with checks or a dedicated credit card. (Many of our friends buy everything they can on a card that provided frequent flyer miles, pay the balance each month to avoid interest, and use the free tickets for a well deserved vacation). This gives you a solid financial paper trail for your accountant and tax filing in the future. You and your accountant may set up a specific list of account categories for your expenses. It is helpful to give each account a code and to put that code on each check and in the check register. This is a good practice for both checks and deposits.

Insurance

There is a basic principle I learned in my years of working in a large corporation; _never risk a lot to save a little._ It makes sense that you would want to purchase insurance immediately. You will need liability and workers compensation. Make certain the rate classification the insurer uses are not their standard restaurant rates. The risk of loss in a coffee house is dramatically lower than in a restaurant.

It may also be wise to have other forms of protection like theft and property protection. Please discuss this with your accountant and insurance professional.

I just cannot help myself, here comes another one, "Only the rich can afford to buy cheap, because they can afford to buy again".

> A Davidism:
> Never risk a lot
> to save a little

The best insurance against the risk of failure is to compete on quality. Buy good value and deliver good value for a fair profit. Employ experts with proven expertise in this specific industry whether it is training, legal, real estate or other. Hire quality people and treat them well. "Hire attitude and train for technique", is a good friends advice. Almost everything I have ever done for short-term gain has cost more in the long term than I was satisfied to pay. I have not seen this admonishment fail in forty years of business, *never risk a lot to save a little*. Please, apply this advice to every buying decision you make as you start up your new business.

Suppliers and Inventory

Look over again what you wrote to describe how your business will operate and the products you will sell. Make a list of the types of companies you will need to purchase from and begin to solicit from them competitive quotes. When you select a supplier, create a list of those individuals and their phone numbers. You will want these numbers with you at all times, and in your store resource manual where everyone knows to find them because you cannot predict when you might need something quickly. All of this information should be posted in the appropriate section of your log and moved into your resource manual later.

Make certain to put in place an accurate, yet easy to follow, procedure for recording your incoming inventory. You should try to develop a simple method of knowing when to order so that your re-supply arrives before you run out of something. Humans are eminently lazy creatures, and since that includes you and me, it is important to establish simple procedures that prevent people from taking or using the last of anything without it having been recorded and re-ordered. Don't simply rely on memory or scraps of notepaper. Be orderly so that you can avoid a crisis during your most inconvenient times.

Daily Recording of Activities

This is a more formal record than your personal log. There are many products for sale at your local office supply store that address this type of accounting, from computer programs to spiral notebooks. But with experience, you might learn to create a better, more comprehensive one yourself.

It is important that you be able to understand what is selling and where you are developing your profits. This means you need to know what things cost you, how much of what you are selling and how much you are giving away for business development. It also is important to know how much is being lost in waste or possibly theft. When you have this data, it will be easier to analyze how your business can be made to grow more profitably.

You can establish a simple but mandatory inventory control process. Whether you employ a simple spiral notebook or put inventory into a computer system, it is critical that you verify every shipment received, record exactly how much product you have on hand by it's most common unit of measure, and how much of your product has left the store daily. It may be easiest to use the same units that the suppliers record your orders in.

Your second step is the recording of your daily sales activity. We have found this is easiest by a combination of counting the material we stock onto the cart each evening or morning and coding the cash register to count our income according to the primary products we sell.

Inexpensive registers are available for around $500, with 8 or 12 keys for coding. In addition you can use the PLU (Price Look Up) feature for other common products. This allows us to use the cash register to count how many flavored Lattes, Mochas, Granita and so on are sold each day. A larger investment into a POS (point of sale) system may be a better idea.

The cups used are counted each day. The number of cups used is then compared to the number of transactions recorded by the register. We also count the units of milk, cream, coffee, cookies, bagels and so on. Taking time the first two months to count and compare these numbers with the register will allow you to establish standard ratios of money taken in to amount of inventory used. This has three powerful benefits for you:

- Your accountant can help you re-compute your business projections and you will then have much more concrete expectations to work with for your own satisfaction and for effective planning.

- When you begin hiring employees, you will have patterns and ratios that will help you determine if your employees are being conscientious about selling, waste control and also determine if they are being honest.

- One of the most important things is to know what is going right so you can do more of that and also to determine what isn't working so you can fix it or eliminate it. Keeping good track of the numbers will allow you to determine what things you cannot afford to have performed incorrectly, as well as those things you are better off delegating to someone else- and things that don't need to be done at all.

I am not very good at managing details, so when I operate a business, I pay all my bills with a check, record the check in the register, put the invoice or receipt into a monthly envelope. At the end of each month I give the accountant a copy of the check register and the envelope. The accountant's assistant enters all this data into a computer and the accountant sends me a monthly profit and loss statement the next day. With the speed of fax systems, this greatly reduces the time I personally spend on paper work so I can concentrate on selling and marketing. Those are the things I do best and the things that won't get done as well by others. Again, these are my A priorities.

Once more, it is very important at the very beginning, to seek the counsel of a reputable small-business lawyer, and an accountant so you have a solid legal, business and accounting structure to grow with.

Further Financial Possibilities

After you know where you will be operating, what the menu will be and have negotiated your rent, you can create a much more personalized financial projection than those we gave you earlier. The following assumptions are taken from the 4-year experience of a company that operates 7 espresso bars.

The steps you need to follow are as follows:

1. What will be the average selling price per transaction?
2. We assumed pastry would account for 10% of total sales on an espresso cart. What percent do you expect? (If you plan to sell bagels, sandwiches, soups, salads or desserts, add the effect of these.)
3. Gourmet coffee averages $1.25 to $1.65 per 12 oz. cup in Minnesota. What will your sizes and prices be?
4. Now compute the total sales for each of these lines. We suggest you calculate sales for 50, 100, 150, 200, 250, 300, and 400 customers per day. How many days per year will you operate?

Cost of goods is computed as follows:

1. Coffee: 8% of espresso and gourmet coffee sales
2. Foods: 9% of total sales
3. Supplies: The biggest contributor here is dairy and paper products 18% to 20%
4. Payroll: Manager wage is computed at $12. Other labor is $7.50.
5. You probably need two people working when demand exceeds 200 customers per day, or 60 per hour. It is unlikely labor should exceed 30% to 33% of gross sales in a mature bar.

Administrative costs:

- Maintenance: We use $50 per month as a cushion.

- Marketing: Seldom have we spent over $200 per month.

- Miscellaneous: This only you can say. We use 2% of sales.

- Benefits: This is usually zero until you have an established business base.

- Rent: Plug in the number that you have agreed to.

- Depreciation: Total up your equipment purchases (usually about $15,000 to $25,000) and depreciate on a 7-year straight line.

- Utilities: Estimate about $200 a month.

- Insurance: Estimate $700 to $1200 a year.

- Actual Insurance: Explore the going rates. With the advent of the Internet you are not limited to using local companies.

Your personal income will be the wages you decide to pay yourself, plus the net income after your debt reduction. You can compute the return on your investment by computing the net income divided by your capital investment and multiply the answer by 100 to determine the annual return on investment.

The three most important questions you need answered at this point are:

- How many customers result in a positive cash flow?

- How many customers do I need to pay myself enough to be excited to go to my own business every day?

- How many customers does it take to achieve both of the above plus 10% or more return on the capital I am investing?

This leads you again to the most important questions...Who are these customers, where are they, how fast can I bring them in? This becomes another extension of your marketing section. Need help? Just call or e-mail. Many sources are free public services. Do not forget your accountant, lawyer, and the expert you've chosen to consult.

Questions:

Are you uneasy about doing the numbers? Hopefully not, but if you are, there are sources for help:

- The Business Plan Disk from **www.thecoffeecoach.net** may help.

- Contact us at **www.thecoffeecoach.net** for help from an experienced advisor.

- You may want to meet with a specialist for one or two days of consulting.

- The local SCORE office may be helpful.

- A discussion with a banker might be quite informative.

TIME OUT

Team Huddle

A business can go in only one direction at a time. Make sure you and your partners have the same business purpose, goals and objectives in mind.

A man and wife pursued opening a drive up coffee and bagel business in a great shopping mall location with a nearly perfect building and great parking. Sounds terrific so far, don't it?

The problem was, this was his idea being funded from proceeds of his construction business, but she was going to run it. What she really liked to do was make pies and she really wanted a wholesale pie making business.

She did everything she could to grow the wholesale part of the business but did nothing to market the retail aspect even though the physical appearance spoke loudly to the public that this was a drive up retail store.

They were out of business within 18 months.

Chapter Seventeen

> Plant a seed every day.
> Nurture it and enjoy the
> season of harvest

<u>Bringing Customers In The Door</u>

With their Money!

Promotional ideas

When opening your business, we recommend a soft opening. Do a lot of promotion for the area residents and other employers around, but do not do a huge *Grand Opening Event* right away. You will learn and work through many little inefficiencies and anxieties the first few weeks. When these are behind you, you can conduct a much larger and more effective grand opening.

When possible, try to arrange for a public interest article in the local paper announcing the future opening of your business. Then invite the reporter to your soft opening and again to the grand opening. This may result in two or three articles. Articles are better than purchased ads, although purchased ads are often very effective. This also will give you two opening opportunities to draw attention.

You cannot give away too many samples in this business. Plan to use a nice tray and 4 oz. cups to serve samples of both gourmet coffee and the espresso drinks. When you first open, try to give a sample to every customer in the mall, every resident in the building or down the block within the first few days. You might consider door-to-door delivering of samples for all the employers you are attempting to draw traffic from. Be sure to sample any bakery, soup and dessert items you may have.

It is effective to give out "2 for 1" cards. We recommend having cards printed on the back of your business card. These "2 for 1" cards should be good for at least 10 to 20 separate days. Our reasoning is that if you can get someone to come back 10 or 20 separate days for a free second drink, you probably have that person hooked as a regular customer.

Most operators will give out frequent buyer cards. These have 10 punch or stamp marks. When the card is filled, the holder gets a drink free.

When people return this card for the free drink, have them sign it with their phone number and address and put it into a drawing. When you enter these names into your computer you have a direct mailing list.

V.I.P. cards can be extremely valuable. Design these to be used with other merchants and employers in the area. *The V.I.P. receives a 10% discount on all drinks served at _____.* In the mall this is given to all employers to give to their employees. Later we simply accept their employee I.D.'s, but in the beginning, you want to create the impression that this is something special you are doing for their employees.

Also encourage these merchants to give out V.I.P. cards to their best customers. Later we will intend to have this same merchant pay for these, but remember in the beginning, we are doing anything and everything to build return traffic, and you cannot get a person to return until after they have already had a rewarding experience!

Ideas that seem to work well in building a growing customer base:

- Provide music. I encourage you to pursue classical or jazz artists. It is something different than they listen to most of the time, it offends almost no one, and somehow it seems to go together with espresso and specialty coffee house atmosphere. Of course there is a certain nostalgic fondness for the coffeehouse folksinger. Base your music choices on your clientele.

- Create a special discount each week for different groups of potential customers. Everyone likes to be special. Perhaps it is employees of specific employers in your neighborhood, members of specific departments if you are in a hospital, the walkers in a mall etc. The idea is to make people special, give them a little discount and over time they will become regulars at regular prices.

- Arrange a few small tables and chairs out of doors; perhaps add one or two umbrellas. Whether you are indoors or out of doors, this European sidewalk atmosphere is very inviting. Be sure to have two or three newspapers handy to encourage visitors to linger, and often, free local publications are a draw to the surrounding readership. They will attract more customers for you.

- Organize an annual calendar of special events; this calendar might also be an effective flyer for your customers to draw them back to the shop later in the month. You want to have some discount special every month. These specials must be timed carefully to gain maximum benefit. The January *NEW YEARS SPECIAL* should be posted immediately after the *AFTER CHRISTMAS* sale. Advertise your *VALENTINE SPECIALS* by January 15. The day following *VALENTINES DAY,* you should post your *ST. PATRICK'S DAY* special and so on.

- Provide educational materials, samples and even classes about the special coffees you are selling. Your market needs to become more educated about the specialty of your products if you expect them to value your products above other alternatives.

- Most operators will offer a small array of pastries. It is good to seek to be different in this regard also. We encourage you to offer fresh *biscotti* in several flavors. This product, specifically designed to be eaten while drinking espresso, is wonderful when fresh and just terrible when made poorly or allowed to become old. Remember: do not serve inferior products.

- You might consider putting in a phone for call in orders, or even a fax. Perhaps offering a delivery service in your building may work.

- When you are serving both espresso and gourmet and flavored coffees, we encourage you to develop the air pot delivery service for employers.

- Always be willing to listen to the customer's wishes and consider adding products. Try formally and informally polling your customers before adding new products. This will help build loyalty by making your customer feel like part of the team.

- Give free drinks on birthdays.

- Some people like to post daily trivia questions. Others put up particular cartoons from a newspaper. Still others select a saying for each day. You are attempting to give customers a reason to make your bar one of their daily habits.

- Prepaid cards are effective for busy people who do not have the time to wait in line. Whether you have these in a card file or on the computer, it is easy to make a drink for that client and eliminate the need for them to carry money. This is particularly effective on campus and in health care institutions where many people do not carry a purse or wallet with them.

- Be creative. Everything is okay to try. Use good humor and good taste. Your customers will enjoy the lighter environment and come to reward your creative efforts.

Half Time

Let's Review

At this point in the book you have:

- Assessed your abilities, attitudes and interests to consider and answer the question: *"Is coffee the business for me?"*
- Been led through the basic steps that must be taken in creating a business plan and strategy.
- Read how to organize, manage employees and attract customers.

You are, at this moment, largely prepared to write a solid business plan, but I encourage you to continue reading through Section Four before doing so.

The following chapters will help you understand how to implement your plan while progressing forward into a profitable business that you *enjoy* owning!

You need:

- A place.
- A good design.
- Health Department approvals.
- Equipment and training.
- Product knowledge.
- Supplies and inventory.

Section IV

Work Your Plan

TIME OUT

Team Huddle

It is easiest to succeed when you are clear about what you wish to do and you have a plan you are following to get you to that end.

A woman had a really good plan to create a Norwegian gift store and coffee shop in a high-income upscale suburb where there were thousands of middle and advanced age residents. A good idea and an ideal target population it seemed.

Although she did not have a signed lease on the perfect small building on one end of downtown, just a conversation with the leasing agent, she began buying and ordering things. One day the space she had chosen in the commercial district was leased to another. Her reaction was to become angry first and then desperate to find another site.

My efforts to keep her calmly focused on her plan failed. She did not want to hear my perception of reality; she wanted things to be the way she wanted things to be.

Here is where she went awry. Desperation drove her to lease a space in a strip mall in the next suburb (A very different environment then originally planned) where the population mix was entirely different. This community was populated by the rapidly rising gen-X young families in their twenties and thirties. A lot of medium to high disposable income sources, with absolutely no nostalgic interest in the Norwegian culture and its ancestors.

Failing to alter her plan to fit the new environment, our friend leased space for the gifts and coffee. She then failed to advertise or market herself to her original target population just a few miles away. Almost no one frequented the gift part of her business. Eventually she turned half of the store into child play area and conference room, but that did not increase her revenue enough to offset the high monthly lease costs and finally two years later she closed the doors.

Her lament in a published interview was, "I wish someone could tell me where I went wrong." Is the answer clear to you?

Chapter Eighteen

Selecting A Location

Research Is The Key

Landlord Summary

LOCATION!
You can make it or
break it

A while back, I ran a survey looking into the attitudes and opinions of the people who managed several of the metropolitan business offices. Fifteen landlords were asked to participate and only one did not have an espresso bar. My primary information results included:

- 80% of the respondents contract with independent operators for their espresso cart operation.

- Recognition of value of experienced consistent specialized operation and management of the cart business. Appreciation of a highly skilled Barista will improve drink sales.

- Improved public relations and perceived extra benefits for employees and building tenants and their guests.

- Incremental new revenue often from space that previously was not revenue producing.

- Carts managed by the landlord or their food service reported a lower per capita market penetration.

- Importance of continuous marketing throughout the year to grow the average daily cup volume.

- Recognizing the value of no hassles, no employee responsibilities, no investment or incremental costs when using an independent contract operator.

You can use these results to tailor your sales approach to various landlords.

Site Evaluation and Planning

As you may know-there is a specialty coffee craze spreading all across this nation. People everywhere are seeing the tremendous potential. This means competitors, both large and small, are going after every location you will go after. How can you succeed ahead of them? *Get there first and arrive with the most professional presentation.* Using a skilled real estate specialist can make all the difference.

What is the first response you are going to get when you begin talking to property managers? Rejection. What is your best weapon? Persistence. This takes focused energy and a time commitment. When you try to negotiate for a premier mall site or a favored office building, you can expect there

> **A Davidism:**
> Get there
> first and
> arrive with
> the most
> professional
> presentation

have been several calls and considerations by your competitors for this same location. What weapon can you add to your persistence? Answer: A professional presentation.

Most people exploring this business spend months evaluating equipment, suppliers, types of coffee, chocolates and so on. They are busy getting comfortable with our industry. They also are cautiously tiptoeing; carefully laying down exactly how they will do their business long before they actually have decided that this is a business they want to do. I understand the pleasure and the frustration of that process because I've done it this way myself. Now I recognize there is a better and much faster way.

Wouldn't it make better business sense to secure a prime area first *and then* diligently explore all those other details?

If most of your competition is busy doing their own kind of research, doesn't that suggest that turning your focus on getting the prime site is a good idea?

Using your local knowledge or a local map, prepare a list of the many different locations you would be interested in. Use the yellow pages to speed your process. On the following pages are some useful ideas that will make your search easier and more successful.

Here are a few helpful hints:

1. If you are fortunate enough to have some influential connection to the person who owns a key site, or someone who heads up the business in that site, by all means use any connections you have to help you on your way. Influence will help ease you into a location faster than any other thing you can do.

If you lack that influence, don't worry about it. The majority of your competitors don't have any influence either. If you are looking for a place in a commercial office building or retail strip mall, you might want to hire a commercial real estate agent to search and negotiate on your behalf.

2. When approaching office buildings, attempt to reach the property manager or director of the building management firm. Often this company is called the *Leasing Agent.* Their name and number can usually be found on the office tenant name board somewhere in the lobby.

3. In large malls, you will usually be looking for the *Mall Manager.* Most sizable malls have an administration office. Large mall management companies may not be easy for a fresh new independent to work with. You might find the owner or leasing agent of a strip mall more to your liking. Often they themselves are small business owners.

4. When seeking a site with a particular retail merchant; say a bookstore, grocer or department store, you will usually be looking for the *Store Manager.* While they may not have the authority to grant you a lease, they can usually point you in the right direction.

5. Approaching corporate campuses, colleges, or hospitals is easy. Simply call the chief executive's office. You will usually be greeted by an executive secretary. Be prepared to explain in two or three sentences what you wish to talk about. The secretary will usually be able to tell you which executive officer you'll need to speak to.

When calling the person to whom you've now been referred, it is helpful to use a simple but specific set of words. "I was referred to you from _____ to discuss _____." You might encounter resistance anywhere along the way in your effort to sell yourself, so stay positive.

Often people, who are not as well informed as you now are about specialty coffee, and the benefits in store for the occupants of a building or campus, will simply attempt to brush you off. This is when your salesmanship begins. What is the easiest picture you can paint for this person so that you can sell your process until you succeed? Two examples may help:

1. Lets say you approach a college and you are told that the food service is contracted exclusively to a major national company. *"Great"*, you say. *"Can you give me the name of the director and a phone number please?"*

You can function as a subcontractor to a food service company just as easily as you can with the college. You will most likely find that very few of your competitors have taken this approach. It is not unlikely that this food service manager has no time to develop a specialty food service like espresso and gourmet coffees. It is also likely that their company is making a bottom line profit of not more than 5% to 7% of their gross sales.

When you offer to bring in all the equipment, handle all the supplies, provide staffing, maintenance and cleanup, *and draw more "new" traffic into the food service area,* you should receive a positive response. If you can afford to pay 7% or more in rent, how can this be a bad decision for the food service? They have no investment, no staffing or training hassles and no operational responsibilities. Yet their net profit is greater than their existing business.

2. Now lets say you approached a hospital, and the Chief Administrator or Chief Financial officer is simply too busy to be bothered by something as minor as your new business idea. This could easily be so, when you consider all the pressures they face daily. Before being dismissed, you might suggest that this service you are prepared to offer will bring remarkable customer and employee relations to the hospital and will be greatly appreciated by the medical staff, the patients and their visitors. It might make sense for you to discuss these benefits and operations issues with the director of the hospital service league or foundation. Such a director may be the best person for you to discuss the benefits of your proposal.

What these two examples demonstrate is that there may be several approaches to a single property. The wise and savvy operator will find and exhaust every angle before abandoning a prime location. It is this persistence and creative flexibility that will give you a greater advantage than your competition.

Sample Letter Proposals

Let's assume that you want to open a cart into an office building lobby.

SAMPLE PROPOSAL

Letter addressed to your prospect

Dear_____

On behalf of (your company) I am very pleased to present our proposal for the operation of a gourmet coffee and espresso bar in the _____. You will find our company to be very professional, highly efficient and well experienced in satisfying the needs of our landlord, fellow tenants and most importantly the residents and visitors of your property.

Specialty coffee, served by well trained professionals will be a tremendous amenity to your property. It is likely we will serve as many as 40% of your daily visitors when the bar matures.

Imagine the positive impact that will produce. In addition to these subjective benefits, (your company name) will pay rent for the space used, thereby producing revenue for the property.

Our company was formed with the support of individuals that have been in this specialty coffee business for years. It is our purpose to take the exciting success of specialty coffee from San Francisco, Seattle, New York, Minneapolis and elsewhere to be at least that successful here.

The type of specialty coffee bar we will propose has been successfully operating indoors and on the streets of many cities for more than 20 years. It will be our pleasure to bring this exciting and successful new marketing feature to your property. OUR BAR WILL BE A SPECIAL AND UNIQUE AMENITY TO YOUR BUILDING, WITH NO COST OR INVESTMENT ON YOUR PART.

Sincerely, _____

President of New Fancy Coffee Shop

Can you see how easily this letter would be modified if your desire was to open a store front, or specialty food and coffee counter in this building? Minor modifications also make it useful to a single building owner or strip mall. Let's continue.

What else do you need to say in your proposal?

- Your overall purpose.
- Why do you want to start this business?
- The opportunities that exist, supported by objective assessment of traffic volume, product and price acceptance, competition, etc.

What will you sell, how much, to whom, and what profit objectives will you accomplish by when?

Chapter Nineteen

Whatever Works

Leasing Hints

I've said previously that one of the keys to success is to *secure* a good location, *develop* that location and *protect* it from the competition. The lease you are about to negotiate will determine much of your ability for all three of these.

The lease will govern how you gain access to customers, your ability to market and promote, and the products you can sell. Now is a good time to know what lawyer you will rely upon.

We began our retail business program using leases based upon a percentage of gross sales from coffee carts. This enables us to pay increased rent as our sales grow, but it avoids a multi-year commitment to a fixed monthly expense. It is slightly negated in that your rent grows as your profit margin expands. You should always plan ahead to a fixed point where your rent will cap and make sure that it is included in your contract or agreement.

This approach has disqualified us in some buildings where the property management insisted upon a fixed monthly rental rate. What this may mean to you is that being prepared to pay a fixed monthly rate will give you a competitive advantage over someone else. If you're renting a fixed number of square feet for a fixed location, you will most likely be paying a fixed rent.

If you rent space in a mall, consider a clause that allows you to vacate without penalty if a major tenants vacates or goes out of business.

Our leases thus far have successfully avoided the usual "triple net" provisions. A property agent may quote you rent as $14.95 a foot, with a $5.50 triple net. Always ask the agent to give you their best estimate of your total annual cost to occupy for the life of the lease. You can then divide by 12 to determine your monthly cost.

If you cannot accomplish the elimination of the "triple net" you may at least be able to put a cap on the costs the landlord can charge. If you are not renting "in-line" space, your small bar or kiosk would be unfairly burdened by the usual triple net provisions and that could mean the difference between profit and loss initially.

We always attempt to include an exclusive and a non-compete clause in our agreements. This may work against you if you are trying to enter a mall or complex where someone else already serves gourmet coffee or espresso. The non-compete clause is included so that we have some protection against a landlord who might wish to terminate our agreement after we have suffered through the start up costs and labored to build customer flow.

Term is important. Renters generally agree to open within a fixed number of days after the landlord has provided the essential power and water access. Our rent being based upon sales volume doesn't begin until sales begin. This might not be true if we had a fixed monthly rental rate.

Many landlords have insisted upon 12-month contract terms. We have responded with a clause that automatically renews the agreement for successive 12-month terms unless the agreement is canceled for cause by notice 90 days before the end of the term.

You also will want an option to renew. Long-term leases are important when you are considering capital investments, and they also make your business more saleable after you have built up a favorable clientele.

It is critical that you know what limitations the lease will impose regarding products sold, signage, promotion to other building occupants, hours of operation and penalty provisions.

When rent is based upon gross sales, it is important that the landlord have a right to audit your books. It is also important that you have reasonable notice, say 30 days. Make sure you have the right to assign your lease. This will enable you to sell the business more easily if you decide to.

It is a good idea to include an arbitration clause, and to spell out the county and state wherein the dispute will be governed.

There are locations where the cart or kiosk operator pays no rent except a stipend to cover electrical expense. The cart or kiosk is an attractive traffic draw to many situations. It may be perceived so valuable by some management, that rent is a non-issue for them. It is always a wise approach to ask if the space will require payment of rent.

Most of the time, these ideas are not going to mean anything to the management you are negotiating with. The site may be in such high demand that you face a "take it or leave it," demand from management.

This is when you really need the advice of an experienced lawyer. You do not want to become so enamored with one particular site that you accept lease terms that will destroy your business. On the other hand, clauses that scare you may in fact not be a real threat at all. Your lawyer should be able to help you evaluate the business risks so you can make an intelligent decision. Not involving a lawyer at this point may be regretted later.

It is valuable to learn to look more closely at what you have left than it is to focus on what you are paying the other party. An example may again be helpful: Lets assume you have one operation selling product at an average price of $1.75 per cup and you pay 10% of sales in rent. Now you have another opportunity to rent space where you can charge an average price of $4.00 per cup but are expected to pay 35% rent. In the first location, you keep 90% of $1.75 or $1.58. In location two you keep $2.60. Location two will pay you more profit than location one.

Most operators prefer a fixed monthly rent. If the amount is an affordable portion of your sales volume, and you have been successful in capping the usual add-on provisions so you know the true monthly rent, there are many advantages to this arrangement. You get to keep more of every new dollar of sales, because as your sales grow your rent remains fixed.

One other very important advantage is that your landlord does not know how much business you are doing. This means you can keep that information confidential. If no one but you know your sales volume, it is going to be more difficult for some competitor to attempt to push you out and replace you by taking advantage of the client base you have established.

One of the most frustrating issues in seeking opportunities to build the espresso business has been the lack of understanding by property managers. Seattle, Portland, NY, LA, Miami and other large cities have malls with as many as ten or eleven espresso operators all successfully conducting business. Many mall managers elsewhere in the country however will say to you, "We already have one coffee store here, and we do not want to violate our loyalty to them or risk their business by introducing a competitor"

It seems that in the case of coffee there simply is no such thing as too much quality competition. Quality vendors of coffee simply speed up the process of educating the public and expanding the market for everyone.

While I respect the mall management's desire to protect the existing tenants, it also seems a little contradictory to me that a mall with 12 or 15 shoe departments would think more than one or two specialty coffee vendors is too many.

One clever way to avoid rent is the espresso bar catering business to private or corporate occasions. It is common to charge $300 to $800 per night for all the drinks the guests care to order for a three-hour event. This would produce a very attractive net profit even if you operated only 3 or 4 occasions per week because you would pay no rent and would rarely need any paid help. If each occasion generated between $120 and $200 in profit, consider the hourly income a 4-hour work shift produces.

The key issue concerning rent is to have thoroughly analyzed the site you want to occupy and know in terms of straight monthly rent (a fixed dollar amount each month) and as a percentage of gross sales what the site is worth to you. Then attempt to negotiate the best deal you can. Your CPA and your lawyer can be tremendously valuable in this part of your planning process.

Chapter Twenty

Health Department Approval

You can't fight city hall!

Don't forget that you will need a license to operate your business. This means you need to comply with environmental health regulations at each site. Health regulations may vary from community to community or in different counties. Generally speaking, the following steps will be an effective beginning.

Call the county Environmental Health Agency to obtain a copy of the regulations you need to comply with. We can help you interpret these.

Before meeting with a health department official you need a plan for that person to review. Demonstrating this level of understanding and consideration will often cause the official to be somewhat more helpful. When you have taken your time to prepare a reasonably complete plan, the official knows you are not wasting time.

The plan should begin with three basic categories:

MENU. What products will you sell? Which will you buy prepackaged and which will be made on site? How will they be dispensed?

EQUIPMENT: Bring a complete list of the equipment you will be using. It will be most helpful if you have a specification sheet for each major piece of equipment. This spec sheet is usually the sales literature from the manufacturer. Health officials are often particularly interested in knowing if a laboratory tested the equipment to comply with certain standards. ETL and UL are the most common electrical safety certifications. Many food-handling items must meet NSF (National Sanitation Foundation) standards and be certified by ETL, UL or NSF.

LOCATION PLAN: Where will you operate? How will food be prepared, stored, dispensed? Where will you store your back up supply of milk, etc? How will employees wash hands, utensils, and equipment, both during the daily operation and at the end of the day?

Most health regulators will require you to have daily access to a clean room or a commissary. This is a sanitary room where food equipment is stored on NSF approved shelving, there is a mop sink for dumping waste water, a triple stainless steel sink for sanitary washing of food handling equipment (large enough to fully immerse the largest piece of equipment you need to wash) and an NSF approved cooler for storing food and milk.

Chapter Twenty-One

Go *With* Flow

Your Design and Layout is so important we address it twice in this book!

The design and layout of every coffeehouse is likely to be unique to each space and it's individual owner. Coffee houses range in size from 500 square feet to about 3,500 feet.

A few basic consumer-related issues need to be taken into consideration:

- What will attract customers?

- How can we make the customer flow smooth and efficient?

- How should products and impulse purchase items be displayed so the customer cannot overlook them?

- Bathroom requirements vary by city and the amount of customer seating involved. Similarly, the number of seats may also influence parking requirements.

- It is preferable to install espresso machines so customers are not staring at the server's backside.

- Designs that allow the coffee brewer and espresso machine on the same counter make it easier to install and use one water filter and water softener configuration.

- Placing the under counter refrigerator below the espresso machine with cup dispensers directly along side the refrigerator make drink preparation more efficient. Positioning it one body width to one side is even better because then one can open the door without moving aside each time.

- Ice machines must have direct access to a floor drain. Ice machines may need a dedicated water filter and softener.

- The espresso machine can be drained to the floor drain. Often it is better to connect to a sink drain. The plumber can install a drain section with a connection similar to one used for a disposal so the machine drain can be slipped over and secured by you or your equipment installer.
- Health authorities often insist upon 3 compartments or 4 compartment sinks. Sinks must be stainless steel NSF certified. An alternative is a commercial NSF rated dishwasher. Sometimes you still need a rinse sink or a dipper well.
- Each work area is also required to have a hand sink with nailbrush, cleaner and towels. You may also need a floor mop sink.

There are several planning steps that will help the new owner:
- Beginning with the floor plan of your space, determine generally what you want the feel and decor to be.
- Next you want to design the working area. We have working relationships with professionals who design coffeehouse interiors. Their computer scale drawings often help you make critical decisions with more confidence and result in more income from your business.
- You need to understand the requirements of your health department.

It is helpful to meet with the health department long before you are prepared to write a formal plan. This meeting allows the inspector to assist you in shaping the formal plan so their plan review goes faster.

The menu you decide upon will help to determine the type of equipment you select:

- Pastry can be displayed in many ways. Individually wrapped in open baskets, on racks or pans within display cases that protect foods from contamination, or if the product contains hazardous ingredients (Cheesecake for example) a refrigerated case may be necessary. Refrigerated cases cost from $2,000 to $8,000 while non-refrigerated may cost from $150 to $1,800.

- Serving freshly baked cookies, muffins and other pastries will give you a tremendous advantage. This can be done in many communities with a small counter top convection oven and no exhaust hood. There are many quality suppliers of frozen dough.

- Many new owners start by purchasing pastry from a wholesaler.

- Recently manufacturers have developed affordable ovens that combine microwave & convection. Now you can bake from scratch without an exhaust hood if you wish not to do the same frozen program everyone else is doing.

- It is becoming increasingly difficult to use stainless pitchers for cream or milk at the condiment counter. A new NSF cream dispenser solves this problem.

- Sandwiches may be created by you or purchased pre-made and may be served cold or hot. One method for a major increase in revenue and profit is the use of a Pannini grill. Pannini is the Italian word for sandwich. These grills ($1,000 to $1,600) enable coffee houses to serve highly unique and highly profitable hot sandwiches, without a hood.

- Making your own sandwiches produces higher profits, but this also requires much more initial investment to meet codes.

- Soup also can be a special attraction in many instances. Frozen soups may be purchased from numerous quality suppliers. A hot plate and two or three compartment serving unit can be added to your store for less than $500.

- Granita, a frozen slush is tremendously popular in fruit flavors but even more as a frozen mocha. Smoothies, blended fruit based drinks, can be efficiently created with a heavy-duty bar blender.

- Special NSF approved shelving will be required for storing your surplus coffee, paper products, and other food handling items.

- Soda water for Italian sodas can be purchased in cans or bottles, but doing so costs about $.35 to $.40 per drink, consumes refrigeration and shelf storage space, while adding to your trash and litter. Using a counter top water charging unit lowers the cost to under $.10 and may be a better approach.

- Fruit flavored teas have become unbelievably popular in recent years. Selling these in bottles or cans will make you very little money, while selling them individually made will be highly profitable. Special tea brewers and dispensers may be a good investment. All the many new Chai teas are also important to research and consider.

Bulk Coffee Considerations

The decision as to whether or not you wish to sell bulk coffee is ruled essentially by:

- Your personal preference
- Your target market
- Store type and space available
- Staffing
- Profitability

The extra equipment you will need is likely limited to bulk bean bins and an approved retail digital scale. You can begin with as few as 8 to 10 coffee varieties. Each region or community will have some variation in what coffees are most popular.

A little research in existing coffee stores to survey the types of coffee and amounts sold will help you make your selections. Often it is much easier to simply meet with the one or two local roasters you will be working with and take their counsel.

I suggest displaying your bulk beans near the store front, in clear bins with colorful informative labels. Clean these bins before adding coffee every time coffee is added.

Bulk beans are so readily available these days that the volume sold from coffee houses are markedly diminishing. This means you must put more energy into communicating and selling to your customers why they benefit from buying beans in your store.

- Display your beans differently than the grocery chain does.
- Keep your beans fresh, less than 7 days old in the bin.
- Clean the bins every week.
- Grind coffee to match each customers needs.
- Sell beans in small quantities.
- Hold a coffee cupping once a month to help educate your customers about specialty coffee.
- Offer specialty gift packaging.

These are just some of the ways you can compete against the large chains to sell more beans.

Chapter Twenty-Two

<u>Preparing To Open</u>

> **Simple preparation can prevent reparation**

Site Prep

Your espresso machine will need to operate on a level surface capable of supporting 150 pounds. The machine requires clearance of at least 1" behind and 3" in front. The surface will need one or two 2-inch holes for hoses and electrical lines to pass through.

If your espresso machine will be plumbed directly to a water supply, you need a 3/8-inch line with a shut off valve within 5 feet. It is important to add a water filter system on this line. Always test the water hardness before installing. Manufacturing warranties won't cover damage from accumulated scale caused by excess minerals in your water. Hardness levels 6 grains or more require a softener.

The coffee brewer and espresso machine are most easily installed if they are on the same surface utilizing a common filter system.

When using a cart (employing water tanks), this filter need should be satisfied at the place where you will fill your tanks. Water is so different from one community to another, that it is suggested you check with local water company for resources to help you select a good filter for your location.

Most health departments require that any espresso machine connected directly to a water line requires a drain, preferably directly under the machine. The logic is the drain needs to be greater than the water supply. This is why a cart drain tank is 6 or 7 gallons and the fresh water tank is 5 gallons.

I will almost never recommend that people purchase 110 volt two group machines. The recovery time on this type machine is too slow. When a two-group machine is needed, always buy a 220-volt unless there simply isn't power available to be pulled to your machine.

When purchasing a cart, insist the cart manufacturer equip it with quick connects for all water connections. These are spring loaded metal and plastic connectors on the water line, the pump and/or the air compressor.

Before your equipment arrives, confirm that you have, at your location, the proper power and plumbing fixtures installed and available. If your service company brings equipment to your store and there is no water or electricity, they cannot install and test your machine much less teach you how to use it. You can expect them to charge you full price for the second trip to your store. Always double-check your power source.

A 220-volt electrical receptacle with proper amperage is required within 4 feet of where you want the machine installed, except when you have purchased a 110-volt unit. Remember you also need 110-volt outlets for the bean grinder and potentially one for a pump if you are installing your machine where you do not have a direct water supply.

Automatic espresso machines may experience difficulty holding the program if voltage and amperage fluctuate too much. This has been a problem with a number of cart operators because many modern buildings are being constructed with only 208-volt lines. When other uses in the building drag the 208-volts down below 200, your espresso machine will begin experiencing difficulty. We now suggest all carts intended for automatic machines consider adding a power booster to assure a true 208 volts or better is delivered to the machine. This inexpensive solution may also solve similar problems in kiosks, stores and coffee shops.

Coffee shops, stores, coffeehouses, and restaurants or cafeterias most often have the espresso machine hooked directly to a 3/8-inch water line. When direct water and floor drains are not available, we will install the machine with a water tank, pump and waste tank just like we do in carts.

Always install a quality water filter. Softeners are used whenever hardness exceeds 6 grains. Under no circumstances do you want to use softened water for coffee brewers. It is widely written that artificially softened water exchanges calcium ions for sodium. This causes over extraction

When your water filter is installed, make sure a drain tap is installed between the filter and the machine so you can flush water through each new replacement cartridge. New cartridges often require five minutes of water flow to activate the carbon filter process.

Your espresso machine should come with an installation guide containing many more specifics about the connections, programming, pressure settings and so on. Each machine is manufactured with a few little differences. Providing you more generic information here would not be very helpful.

The single largest error that new owners commit is: failing to set aside several hours of undivided attention to their initial training. Ninety percent of all machine problems with service are due to operator error or lack of understanding the machine. These may all be avoided with more concentrated training time and concentration when your equipment is installed.

Training

Plan to spend two to four hours on your first installation. These hours are much more valuable for you if you've read this book and your owners manual thoroughly beforehand and have also viewed the training video we furnish.

In addition to installing and testing your machines, the service person can usually help you understand how to use, clean and maintain it. I highly recommend that new buyers contract to have Preventive Maintenance on each machine every 90 to 120 days. A comprehensive Preventative Maintenance plan can avert almost all unexpected interruptions of service, leaving you free to always serve customers and take in money.

SECTION V

Rounding Up The Little Things

Chapter Twenty-Three

Product Preparation

The Nuts And Bolts Of Product

Development

There is no substitute for quality

How Do You Choose a Roaster?

My highest admiration goes to roasters who have dedicated years to the science and art of coffee roasting, yet humbly and readily admit how much there is still to be learned.

It is easy for dishonest roasters to be misleading and fraudulent about the quality of the coffee they offer. The coffee market is much too competitive for any roaster to offer premium quality coffee at prices markedly different than other roasters, so select your coffee supplier on reputation, integrity, consistency, ability to help you market and the quality of taste. When you do a tasting, ask 8 or 9 friends to participate so you have a consensus to start from.

First, contact the SCAA to see if the roasters that you are considering are members in good standing of this organization.

Second, personally interview the actual roaster and do a walking tour of the roasting facilities. Does your roaster love his job? Is his workspace orderly and clean? How well is the green coffee stored? What sort of, if any, educational material is available for you and your future customers?

Third, interview a list of the roaster's customers *and* their customers. How is the roasters customer service? How much do the end users like the product?

Last, and I do mean last, do a price/value comparison.

Specialty coffees sell best when brewed directly into and served from commercial air pots or thermal insulated containers. Coffee brewed directly into thermal containers and quickly sealed, holds taste and temperature well up to 3 hours.

Some coffee brewing basics to share with your customers include:

- **BUY WHOLE BEANS** in a quantity you will use within a week of opening the bag.

- **DO NOT STORE COFFEE IN THE REFRIGERATOR** or for that matter the freezer. Keep coffee dry, sealed from air and light.

- **DON'T SKIMP.** Cheating on the correct amount to produce the best taste is a sure way of contributing to your own failure.

- **GRIND YOUR COFFEE FRESH** and grind it at the correct setting for your brewer.

- **NEVER BOIL COFFEE.** Coffee brews most effectively between 194 and 205 degrees. Cowboy coffee is only for camping trips and with the ease and availability of French Press coffee brewers it is entirely superfluous.

- **NEVER REHEAT COFFEE.** All coffee becomes distasteful after only 10 to 20 minutes of constant heat.

- **ALWAYS USE COLD WATER.** Do not use softened water from a salt-based system to brew coffee.

- **NEVER REUSE GROUNDS.** After one brewing, the only thing left is waste, bitter oils, acids and unpleasant taste. It makes great compost

Making Espresso Drinks

Okay, let's get back to work on your machine. Would you like to make a drink on your new machine? Good, let's begin.

While this business seems very complex, it can be reduced to a few fundamentals making it easier to understand. First, understand that espresso machines only produce either a single or a double shot of espresso. Second, you can steam milk with your espresso machine. Third, you can often get hot water from your espresso machine. That's about it. Making espresso drinks is an art form and the above listed three things are the tools that you will use to make that art. It's that easy, except not really.

1. Remove the double pour portafilter. This is the one with the pour spout with two outpouring openings. Place the portafilter end into the guide on your grinder and pull the dispensing lever twice. If you had ground enough coffee to permit a full measure of coffee with each pull, you will now have two 7-gram measures of coffee in the portafilter. This gives you a level full basket before tamping.

2. Tamp this coffee into the filter basket with either the tamp device on the grinder, or your hand tamp. Wipe any excess coffee off the rim of the portafilter and then place the portafilter into the group head. Fit it into the alignment notches and give it a firm, but not overly hard, tightening twist to the right.

3. Place your cup or brew pitcher under the pour spouts and push the control button. On an automatic machine, you push the button with a picture of two shots of espresso. Semiautomatics require you to push the brewing button to begin the water flow and push it again later to stop it.

4. Automatic machines will electronically shut off the flow of water when the programmed amount of water (usually 2.5 ounces for a double) has passed through the coffee.

5. When you use a semiautomatic machine, you have to continue to observe the brewing and re-push the brew button when the proper amount of water has passed.

6. If *the coffee has been properly ground and tamped into the* portafilter, your brew process should have taken between 18 and 25 seconds. You should have

about 2.25 oz. of espresso, including a rich, caramel colored "crèma" on the surface.

7. While the machine is brewing the espresso shots, take your pitcher of non-fat milk out of the refrigerator and fill it about 1/3 full of milk. Make sure it is not more than half full of milk; because the milk and froth almost double when you finish.

8. Open the steam valve briefly to blow out any condensed water and re-close. Place the pitcher under the steam wand so the steam openings at the tip of the wand are immersed just under the surface of the milk. Hold the pitcher at a slight angle. Open the steam valve fully. After creating an inch or two of foam, immerse the wand deeper into the milk to continue steaming it to the right temperature, (between 150 and 160 degrees). If you stop frothing when the thermometer reads 140, the milk temp will almost always be between 152 and 155. You may soon learn to judge this by feel; but we prefer you be more precise by using a thermometer that clips to the side of the steaming pitcher. Shut off the steam valve when finished, _before_ removing the pitcher.

9. Immediately wipe down the steaming wand with your damp bar towel (used exclusively for this purpose). Release a blast of steam to blow out any milk that was drawn into the wand when you shut off the steam.

10. When the steam pressure is turned off, it is replaced with an instant vacuum that draws milk up into the steam wand. If you fail to blow this out, the milk can harden and interfere with further steaming of the next drink. It may result in very adverse taste consequences in future drinks or even cause boiler contamination. You can quickly understand why this steam wand cleaning step is so important.

11. I like to bang the pitcher once or twice on the bar top to cause the foam to settle. Then pour milk to about half inch from the top and cap off with a generous layer of firm foam. There you have it, your first Latte.

Now that you understand the machine and know how to make espresso-based drinks, let's take some time to talk about coffee and profitable recipes you can begin with.

Espresso Standards

True espresso is made by forcing water heated to approximately 195 degrees F. at a pressure of around 9 atmospheres (about 132 p.s.i.) through finely ground coffee. This produces a concentrated, aromatic and highly flavorful extract, which truly is the "heart" of coffee.

The coffee beans you use should have been carefully blended and specifically roasted for espresso.

Following these guidelines will produce *Excellent Espresso*

1. Temperature of the brewing water should be between 194 and 198 degrees
2. Boiler pressure (top reading) should be 1.0 to 1.5, line pressure (bottom reading) 9.0 atmospheres during the brewing process.
3. Use coffee within one hour of grinding. If you have old coffee, throw it out.
4. The proper dose level is 7 grams for a single shot of espresso.
5. Every shot should be served and/or mixed within ten seconds.
6. A single shot should be approximately 1.25 oz. including crèma.
7. Brew time should range from 18 to 25 seconds.
8. For consistency purposes, *always* make espresso into a warmed cup, unless you're using a to-go cup.

Always make an effort to explain your actions to your patron.

You are serving a highly customized drink to your customers. The equipment allows you to tailor every drink to fit the taste of every customer. There is no need to pass up this wonderful opportunity. Attempt to get customers to tell you in detail what they like so you can make their special drink their way. If your drink doesn't meet their standards all your efforts are for naught.

Freshness standards

Coffee- Your supplier should provide helpful guides to assure you are producing the best drink from that coffee. I prefer to receive my coffee in bags with flavor lock seals. Coffee will remain fresh for many weeks after roasting in these bags. It is important to mark your coffee by date to rotate product so coffee will not grow stale.

Milk- your dairy needs to be purchased and delivered almost daily for most cart operations, but much less frequently in others.

- It is important to watch the dates and rotate stock correctly to avoid old product.
- Store milk between 35 and 40 degrees.
- Check the temperature, rotate stock, and make sure your refrigerator has good air circulation.
- Do not use milk that has been frozen. It will not foam.
- The milk types used in espresso bars include: whole, 2%, 1%, non-fat and half & half.
- The steaming pitcher should always be returned to the refrigerator after every drink if it is not going to be used promptly for the next person in line.
- It is important to keep extra pitchers on hand (at least 4 total). Some health authorities require frothing pitchers be cleaned and sanitized every 2 hours.

- Keep the foam knife and spoon in a running dipper well.
- Milk is the part of your product called "potentially hazardous" that makes the health department people so cautious. Do yourself a favor; learn to be fussy about milk cleanliness.

Steaming and foaming

Milk is *steamed* for Café Lattes, mochas and hot chocolate. It is *foamed* for Cappuccinos and Macchiatos. Foaming is more challenging than steaming.

- To foam milk for a cappuccino, start with a clean pitcher filled about 1/3 with cold milk.
- Hot milk won't foam.
- Place the steam wand just under the surface and fully open the steam valve.
- As the foam rises, lower the pitcher until you have created the desired level of foam.
- Keep watching the temperature of the milk (always remember to use a food grade thermometer) so you do not overheat it.
- Your espresso equipment supplier or your roaster should be able to provide you with hands-on training for milk steaming.

Steam Wands

Always remember how important your steam wands are. It is impossible to over-emphasize the importance of proper cleaning and maintenance of your equipment. Experienced service technicians have told me well over 80% of the repair service calls they receive are due to operator error; and 90 % of those have to do with cleaning and routine maintenance especially that associated with managing water conditions and filtration.

Blast steam from the wand *before* using every time. This will prevent you accidentally drawing milk into a cold boiler that had a vacuum in it when you or your employee thought it was hot and pressurized but it wasn't.

You cannot take too much care in cleaning anything that contacts milk. Wipe the steam wand after every drink with a bar towel used exclusively for that purpose.

If the steam wands are not cleaned and blasted free of milk after each drink, you may develop a blocked steam wand. We suggest putting the wands into a small cup or pitcher with hot water each night before leaving. Next morning, rinse and wipe clean the wand, blow it out with steam, and it will be fresh and clean to begin each day.

Periodically water may begin to drip from around the steam wand connection. This means the connection is loose, or the little "O" ring inside has worn. It is a simple procedure to remove the steam wand and replace the "O" ring when the machine is cold.

You may notice dripping from the tip of your steam wand sometime in the future. This or a small steady flow of steam leaking from the tip means the rubber seal inside the steam valve needs to be replaced. Call for instructions, or to arrange a service call when your store is not so busy. This will avoid a crisis for you at some later date.

Listening to customers, being creative and having fun produces success. Another component you need is a simple yet varied menu.

Espresso Based Drinks

Espresso and the drinks made from it are the most successful featured drinks for most bars and coffeehouses, but selling strictly espresso in any U.S. business would make financial success difficult. Café Latte, Cappuccinos and Mochas may be your highest margin drinks, but many of your clients often want other drinks available as well.

<u>Coffees and Recipes</u>

Espresso is so named because it is made instantly upon request. Espresso is just one form of creating extraordinary coffee drinks from Specialty Coffee. Coffee plants are evergreen, develop lovely white flowers and produce brilliant red cherries, usually containing two seeds per cherry. Incidentally, when nature produces only one seed per cherry, they're called *Peaberries.*

It may help to know the word *Espresso* has many meanings to different people and at different times. It is:

- A method of making coffee
- A blend of beans
- A degree of roasting
- A drink in a cup

Roasters usually blend a variety of 3 to 6 types of beans to create the taste they are seeking for their particular espresso blend.

Coffee beans of different varieties may be blended before or after roasting. The roaster determines which method to use depending upon the coffee beans being used and the taste to be developed.

During your typical days operation you will use the espresso equipment to produce basically three types of drinks.

Espresso

1 to 1.25 oz. liquid extracted from 7 grams of ground coffee. Less than 10% of customers order straight espresso in most US markets, but those who do usually know very well what they want and have the experience to know quality when they drink it. Often these people order triples and even quads.

Americano

Espresso with water added to fill a cup similar to a typical American coffee-This makes a rich, full bodied, premier cup of coffee, truly the pinnacle of taste. Americanos are nothing short of the finest way to drink a full cup of coffee.

Café latte or Cappuccino

Basically espresso with steamed or foamed milk added. Cappuccino, as a general rule, should be about equal parts milk and foam over the espresso shot. A "dry cap" would be one with almost no milk, just coffee and foam.

Café Latte means coffee with milk in Italian, just as Café Au Lait does in French. The recipe is Espresso, fill the cup with steamed milk to about 1/2 inch from the top and finish with a beautiful crown of snowy white foam.

Knowing these three basics, a barista is now free to create, and create we do. Employing seasonings, chocolate, vanilla powder, a broad range of Italian syrups, alternative types of milk and accentuating garnishes, the drink possibilities are almost endless.

Mocha

Mocha is a Latte with chocolate syrup mixed into the espresso before adding the milk. It is perhaps the most popular flavored latte. Clearly it is so popular it has developed it's own name. Often dressed up with whipped cream and sprinkles.

Flavored Lattes

Lattes flavored with Vanilla, Almond and Hazelnut is next in popularity. When making hot flavored Lattes we suggest beginning with a standard measure of .5 ounce of syrup for a regular (8 oz), .75 ounce for a tall (12 oz) and 1.0 ounce for a Grande

(16 oz.). Ice lattes require more syrup to achieve the same level of flavoring. Why? Heat tends to intensify the flavor components.

Many shop owners now use serving pumps fitted into each syrup bottle. One pump delivers about 1/3 oz, perfect for flavoring an 8oz. drink. One can achieve more consistency with these measured pumps.

Next in popularity seems to be a variety of latte drinks made with two flavors. Raspberry, mint or almond mochas are good sellers. Almost any fruit flavor syrup will blend well with Vanilla or Almond. Some combinations lend themselves to specialty names. Cleverly named drinks will increase their popularity.

Don't forget about iced drinks, especially in the heat. First of all, all iced drinks should be served in glass or clear plastic cups. This enables your customer to appreciate your creation with three senses; sight, feel and taste. The procedure for iced drinks is:

- Add flavoring
- Add cold milk
- Pour in espresso
- Put ice in cup
- Stir

Whipped cream is rarely served on iced drinks. When using plastic cups, have lids available with straw slits.

It may come as a shock to some people in the coffee business, but not everyone likes or drinks coffee. You may still have many of these people as customers. Pretend you have a pair of adult customers and their children at your bar. One orders a Latte. What do you offer the other three? ...Teas, hot moos, Italian soda, granita or a smoothie!

Iced non-coffees

Iced coffee-free drinks are another important part of your menu. The drinks of greatest popularity are two types: Italian sodas and Granita.

Italian Sodas

Italian Sodas are made using the same Italian syrups we have been discussing.

- Fill a cup with ice,
- Add plain charged water, and
- Stir in the flavor desired.

These drinks are often more popular with women and children, but I will always enjoy a good Strawberry/Vanilla soda. Also remember that you can add more flavors, but can't take it back out? The ratios we suggest for sodas are:

- 1 oz for a regular (8oz)
- 1.5 oz for a tall (12oz)
- 2 oz for a grande (16oz)

These drinks are converted to an *Italian Creamosa* by leaving enough room for an ounce or two of milk or half and half. One very popular creamosa is a dreamsicle. This is orange flavoring, soda and half and half. This drink seems to remind many patrons of their childhood memories of the creamsicle with the same name.

Test yourself on the following drink descriptions:

- **ESPRESSO:** Both a drink and a brewing method for coffee using pressurized hot water to extract the full flavor from a ground, specialty "espresso roast" coffee. The extraction should take at least 18, but not more than 25 seconds to produce the best flavor and crème.

- **CAFÉ LATTE:** Espresso with mostly steamed milk topped with a dollop of frothed milk.

- **FLAVORED LATTE:** A latte with a syrup or combination of syrups added, sometimes topped with whipped cream.

- **CAPPUCCINO:** Espresso with equal parts steamed and frothed milk.

- **CAFÉ AU LAIT:** Basically it's half of a cup of coffee topped with milk and foam and served like a latte.

- **AMERICANO:** A shot of espresso with hot water added, a rich full bodied taste.

- **BREVE:** An espresso shot with steamed and frothed half & half.

- **DEPTH CHARGE:** Shot of espresso added to brewed coffee.

- **LUNGO:** An espresso shot pulled "long" to produce a "milder" espresso. This is the "American Standard" way of extracting espresso.

- **ESPRESSO MACCHIATO:** Espresso "marked" or topped with a dollop of thick foamed milk. Serve in a small cup.

- **LATTE MACCHIATO:** Steamed milk "marked" with half the amount of espresso as a normal latte.

- **MIEL:** A breve flavored with honey.

- **MOCHA:** Espresso with chocolate syrup added, steamed milk and topped with whipped cream.

- **MOO OR STEAMER:** Milk steamed to approximately 150-155 degrees, using a thermometer, with the appropriate amount of flavoring added and topped with whipped cream.

- **RISTRETTO:** An espresso shot pulled short, restricting the pour to the most flavorful part.

- **SKINNY:** A latte or cappuccino made with skim or non-fat milk.

- **WHY BOTHER:** A latte made with skim or non-fat milk and decaf espresso.

Specialty Coffees

Specialty coffee sold along with espresso usually means special varieties, such as Sumatra, or individual roasts, such as French Roast, and Arabica coffees flavored, such as Vanilla Nut, by the roaster with special flavoring extracts. These offerings provide wary clients and shy or timid customers a safe pathway to experiment with new tastes. This affords you the opportunity of a relatively easy method to up-sell customers to ever higher levels of enjoying your unique products.

Some purists, by the way, oppose serving flavored coffees. They seem to feel flavoring coffee is offensive. I disagree. The flavoring of coffee dates back hundreds of years. The roaster flavors coffees by adding a measure of extract to a drum of roasted beans. The drum is turned until all of the extract is absorbed into the beans.

Iced Drink Options

When hot weather moves in, all of the espresso based drinks can be served iced. You may also wish to sell Italian Sodas, specialty teas, or the new rage products, Granita or smoothies.

Buzz-Free (Non-Coffee Drinkers Spend Money Too!)

Children and non-coffee drinkers are attended to with "Hot Moos or Steamers" of an endless flavor variety using the same Italian syrups you employ to make flavored lattes. These are made with steamed milk, Italian syrup flavors, spices and whipped cream.

Tea-Time

Teas are now becoming highly popular. This product requires considerable study so your presentation is both appealing and interesting to your clientele. The new fruit juice teas, as well as the Indian Chai teas, are very popular and should not be overlooked as a good profitability resource.

Food, etc.

In the second half of the 90's our industry cleverly utilized new technologies to serve sandwiches, soups, salads and desserts. All of these dramatically increase the average customer transaction, so you can increase profits with fewer customers and less work. Pannini grills are of particular interest. I often call them money printing presses.

Restaurant equipment manufacturers now have developed NSF approved cream dispensers, 3 to 6 pint gelato makers, and combination microwave/ convection ovens to give you more menu options.

I frequently tell clients they are really entering the education and entertainment business. Coffee and tea are merely tools employed the way other artists might utilize instruments or stage props. Menu is important, but perhaps knowledge, consistent quality standards and a desire to entertain and serve others are even more important.

Granita Machines

A granita is a drink chilled and mechanically stirred continuously to maintain a slush consistency. The liquid must have at least 13% sugar and must be kept in motion to prevent it from freezing. This product is popular whether served as a fruit flavor or as a slushed cappuccino.

You can make your own mix, but doing so endangers the safety of your equipment. Some methods of mixing the liquid will allow the fruit flavor to separate from the ice crystals in the glass. This would, of course, result in unsatisfied customers.

Whether or not you choose to make your own or buy commercial mixes, quality and consistency remain the most important factors.

Granita machines are tremendous revenue producers for two reasons:

1. First, the machine keeps the product in motion. This feature seems to cause the product to repeatedly say to the customer "Buy me, Buy me"!

2. Second, the machine will either freeze the liquid or simply chill it. Therefore you can use the same piece of equipment as either a fruit juice or a Granita dispenser.

Chapter Twenty-Four

The Quality Issue Reviewed

Always Take the Time to Do It Right

> **"Anything worth doing is worth doing well"**
> *Mother Evert*

QUALITY is another topic about which numerous authors have written volumes. Perhaps I am remiss in not dedicating an entire section of this book to this subject, but I think others have spoken better on this subject than I can so I again refer you to the SCAA and your local library for books on this subject.

Individually exceptional service and unwavering quality are the two greatest competitive advantages the independent operator has in competing with chains and national firms.

Large firms have support staff, professional marketing departments, public recognition and so on, BUT you have Personal attention of the owner, a unique personality and charisma and the opportunity to manage to the highest standards of quality because you have more direct control. You have everything to gain and nothing to fear from the existence of large national firms who continue to increase the public's awareness about specialty coffee.

Quality begins with an attitude or perspective. Exceptional quality is what your customer perceives it to be not what you think it is. Pay attention to your customers, ask their opinion, sample products Etc.

One of the most important factors in the customer's mind is RELIABILITY. Can I rely upon you? Are you open and ready to serve all of the hours you publicize? Does the coffee taste the same every time I order it. Is it the same temperature? Does everyone make the drink the same way? Are all the drinks and foods fresh and of superior quality?

CONSISTENCY is another major factor. Do you know how to source premium products? Do you understand how to objectively assess the vendors so you are selecting from only the best? Do you understand that cost is the least important factor in everything you buy? (If this statement makes you react defensively or in disagreement, you may already be headed for the world of mediocrity).

CLEANLINESS is so obvious, why does it need to be written about? Because, some operators not only do not clean the bathroom every couple hours, some wait days and even weeks. Dirt and dust is allowed to accumulate in corners, on light fixtures, glass shelves and so on, for days. Syrup bottles are allowed to be sticky. Steam wands are not wiped clean after every drink, coffee bags set half closed on the back counter, product lines show in the bowls of granita machines ETC.

Equipment must be maintained, kept clean, fix or replace things that break or get damaged.

My son taught me a great perspective, "If there is time to lean, there is time to clean".

Coffeehouses cannot be too clean or too orderly!

PRODUCT KNOWLEDGE and a passionate appreciation for great coffee are, in my opinion, absolutely essential. There is no substitute for passion. Customers will return to buy anything you are excited about, proud to serve and passionately interested in. I also frequently tell folks this business is more about educating and entertaining customers than it is about food service. This having been said, it begs the question how does one gain this knowledge and passion?

Educational resources from SCAA.org are again my first referral. Fresh Cup.com is another source for many articles intended to aid independent operators. Gourmet Retailer and Tea & Coffee are other good industry trade journals.

You are going into the coffee business, so it is essential that you learn how to source exceptional coffee. There is more.

How do you store and care for coffee once it arrives? What kind of equipment makes great coffee. There are brewers available today that will deliver as much as

15% to 25% more taste in the cup than others do. Precise brewing control of temperature, water flow rate, and extraction time can now be easily managed, but it requires you buy the better quality equipment.

New equipment ages and as it does, it will continue to produce excellent coffee only if you clean it well every day and keep it well maintained. There are some suggestions in the Resource Manual.

Water makes up over 98% of a cup of coffee. How do you plan to learn how to effectively manage your water quality? The best equipment suppliers can help you.

Putting out a quality product is hard work, but competing on quality is the best way to achieve success. Does it sound like I am advocating perfection? I am not, as that is unrealistic. On the other hand, I abhor being satisfied by equaling or exceeding the performance of another. Passionately pursue your own highest potential and strive for excellence every day and you will be pleased with your accomplishments.

TIME OUT for *A Team Huddle*

I have, for years, been accumulating ideas for my next book. The title is "IT SAYS EASIER THAN IT DOES".

Failing to "walk our talk" or actually creating absolute contradictions in the mind of customers and employees is a trap each of us faces every day.

Few can do this on their own. I found that empowering employees and rewarding them for catching me in my failings helped me achieve more of my potential more of the time. Encouraging and rewarding customers for respectfully informing you when you fail to exceed their expectations is invaluable. Good friends (and your best customers) will tell you what you need to know rather than what you would like to here.

176

Ordering breakfast in a high visibility coffeehouse in Calgary, I saw that the side panel of the espresso machine was duct taped. What message did this give to his employees? If he wouldn't repair such an obvious, inexpensive and unsightly breakage of his most important machine, why should I think that his coffee storage bins, refrigerator or brewers were any better maintained?

In the process of working on a machine, I knocked down a stack of paper cups. The store manager promptly picked them up from the floor and returned them to the top of the machine to be used.

A coffeehouse employee placed a large pitcher of cold milk under the steam wand to steam it and walked away. The screaming noise was so loud patrons had to raise their voices to continue conversing.

Having ordered two double shot lattes, I watched the owner run two ounces of liquid into two separate cups from one portafilter. That is 4 ounces of water through 14 grams of coffee. When I courteously asked her to make two drinks with only two ounces from that same quantity of dosed coffee, she politely did so. Then charged me extra for the shots I declined to drink. "This is how our roaster trained us to make drinks" she advised.

Commenting to a barista, this Sumatra has a little vanilla taste in it, I was told, "Oh that happens because we use one grinder for all our coffee." He revealed no understanding that his coffee was unsatisfying to his customer.

"That is how we make it here" is a phrase no customer ever wants to here. "How would you like me to make it?" sounds better.

Talking on the phone while taking an order or making drinks says, "You are inconveniencing me."

Broken coffee beans or dirty corners in coffee bins say, "You are not smart enough to know real quality from pretense."

177

Permitting any customer to stand in line without acknowledging their presence within 5 to 10 seconds says "I am busy, I'll get to you when I can."

Doing anything in preparation for closing while customers remain in your store says "I wish you would leave already."

Quality is an attitude. Attitude Affects All (The triple A philosophy). People who truly believe and work daily to be AAA operators succeed!

Chapter Twenty Five

The Giant Lists Of Things You Have To Buy

These really are things that you **have** *to buy.*

<table>
<tr><td>The Menu Dictates Your Market</td></tr>
</table>

We've covered just about everything we can possibly cover, as it has to do with Specialty Coffee. We've covered a lot of information between the initial conceptions of your idea to full realization of your business plan. I have done my best to impart you with the fruits of the knowledge tree and the lessons I have learned from making the mistakes that this book should help you navigate around.

Yet, it seems to me that there are just a few little things that you need before you open your doors for business. Your equipment.

As I've mentioned earlier and throughout this book, your equipment is the main and primary revenue maker in your shop. Never, ever, buy a piece of machinery because you found it at an online auction for a steal and it's cheap unless you are prepared to spend a lot more to make the machine work properly. Take the time to research and study the machines and the machine supplier that you will use. Spend the time learning about your machines, their uses and functions and, most of all, their serviceability.

Every machine will break. Therefore *"it is more important who you buy from than what you buy."* (One last Davidism)

Don't be hasty in your excitement. These are the machines that you will be spending an enormous amount of time with. Get something that you feel comfortable with, even if you have to spend more to get it. Quality will always shine through.

With this aside, lets move on to the lists. I have split the following items into two separate, yet equally important parts. Equipment and Ancillary.

Equipment Shopping List

- Espresso Machine
- Espresso grinders
- Bulk Coffee Grinder (two if you use flavored coffee)
- Coffee Brewer
- Air pots
- Ice Machine
- Charged-Water Maker
- Refrigerator
- 3 or 4 Compartment Sink
- Hand sink (size)
- Pastry Display
- Cash Register
- Food Prep Table
- Granita Machine
- Blender
- Pannini Grill ask
- Microwave
- Convection/Micro Oven
- Coffee Bins / bags ?
- Exterior Signs
- Menu Boards
- Tables, Chairs and Umbrellas
- Under counter Dishwasher
- Upright Coolers

- Freezers
- Soup Cooker/Warmer
- Refrigerated Display
- Refrigerated Sandwich Prep

Ancillary Shopping List

- Decaf Coffee Doser
- Shot Pitchers
- Shot Glasses
- Frothing Pitchers
- Thermometers
- Spatulas
- Serving Spoons
- Grinder Brushes
- Knock Box
- PuroCaff
- Coffee Tamp
- 7 Gram Scoop
- Water Filter
- Water Softener
- Cup Dispensers
- Lid Holder
- Syrup Racks
- Syrups and Pumps

- Paper Supplies
- Coffee
- Iced Tea Dispenser
- Anti-Fatigue Mats
- Bar Towels and Aprons
- Cream Whipper and Cartridges
- Transport Cart
- Towel Dispenser and Soap
- Promotional Banner
- Waste Receptacle
- Condiments
- Food Supplies
- Cleaner and Polish
- Shakers for Toppings
- French Presses
- Travel Mugs
- Tongs
- Bleach Bucket
- Rubber Gloves/Plastic Rags
- Short Screwdrivers
- Pliers
- 4" Crescent Wrench
- 3 Toothbrushes and awl
- Dust Pan and Broom

Chapter Twenty Six

Summary

The End
(of the beginning)

Another Personal Letter From THE Coffee Coach

Wow! That was quite a lot to grasp and put to use.

The overall purpose of this book is to help readers reduce the time it takes to open a new business by about six to twelve months and to lower the cost of start-up by several thousands of dollars. The second purpose is to provide a continuing sense of confidence and enthusiasm.

The first objective of this book, addressed in the personal assessment segment, is to help you determine if you really want to start your own business now that someone has shown you most of the reality involved.

Whether you clearly conclude yes or no, we have accomplished our first objective of helping every reader in some way.

Hopefully the section on coffee history and the types of business caused you to grow in excitement as you see how flexible this industry is. There is a way to succeed that fits every one.

The planning section is intended to demonstrate that this is not complicated. It does not need to be overwhelming. You can do this as well as anyone else. If you plan your approach and then methodically implement your plan, starting a coffee business should be fun, exciting and rewarding.

All along the way, I have tried to provide some coaching and mentoring advice that will empower you to create your own game plan and confidently persist into success. I have talked about *Understanding* yourself before going forward, the power of *Attitude,* managing *Risk* through wise purchasing, creating a business built upon a standard set of values all tied to *Quality,* and accomplishing your end objectives through effective *Planning & Methodical patterns.*

At this juncture, I would like to suggest you perform some preparation homework:

First, create a self-assessment like the one we

A Favorite Davidism:

"If you are starting a business, do it to make a difference."

---

discussed earlier and begin filling it in. Keep it with you daily so you can add and change it as ideas come to you. After a week, you should be ready to do a completed one.

Second, I encourage you to find a quiet space and time when you can look into your heart and soul. Close your eyes, look at your coffee business on a very busy day months after you have opened and speak out loud to another person or into a recording device everything your minds eye sees.

What time of year is it? Where are you? What are you doing? Who is there with you? What colors do you see, smells you smell, do you hear music, what are customers doing, are there plants, hanging or standing and so on.

Try to do this without thinking. When finished, transcribe everything, and then do the thinking so you can write a word picture in not more than two sentences that

184

Michael

clearly states your vision and concept. The clarity this will bring to you will enable you to put the picture in your mind into everyone's mind that you need to assist you in realizing this vision.

Third, complete the questions in Chapter 6 and send them to me.

Fourth, take part of one day to write down your answers to the 10 questions in the business plan outline in Chapter 8. When you have written what you know and think you know, your mind will be free to focus on other things you need to add. Also, after writing things down, you can stop thinking about them because they will not get lost, you can always find them when you need to. *612-282-9301,*

cell phone

When you have completed these four steps call 1-800-900-3993 or e-mail **www.thecoffeecoach.net** and I, or one of my associates, will be happy to discuss your plan and any help you may wish.

The Coffee Coach is available to help you in several ways:

- A class, "How to Start a Coffee Business" is conducted frequently in Minneapolis and Chicago. If demand supports doing so, we will bring the seminar to several other cities. Check the web site for dates and packages.

- On the phone consulting for an hourly fee.

- You visit one of our centers for training and consulting. You pay a deposit that is later used to reduce your cost of equipment.

- We visit your site. Your deposit reduces the cost of equipment. You pay travel and per diem expenses.

- Our web site offers several books & videos you may find useful.

- Free referral to key experts:
  - o Designers   *3/20*

- Legal Accountants
- Coffee house licensers
- Espresso equipment vendors
- Ancillary suppliers
- Coffee Roasters

I love this business. I have a passion for helping people grab a piece of the American dream. I enjoy instilling in people a passion for what they can accomplish through coffee. One of my Davidisms is, *"If you are starting a business, do it to make a difference."* You can literally change the world for a lot of people through coffee, and I encourage you to go forth and do so.

David Evert
Minneapolis, MN 2002

P.S. To receive The Coffee Coach Business Planner on diskette, call 1-800-900-3993 or visit **www.TheCoffeeCoach.net.** The planner is free; you just pay the shipping and handling.

Appendix A

Capital Requirements

Before we can begin to assess what equipment we need or how to design and construct our facility, we must decide what we will serve and how it will be prepared. Refer to the menu provided later in Appendix B before making your decisions. Some ball park estimates include:

Espresso machine, one or two grinders	$7500
Coffee brewer, servers & grinders	$2500
Two or three sinks	$1500
Single LJ/C refrigerator	$1300
Upright cooler	$1500
Dry pastry case, floor model	$1500
Cold display case (NSF)	$6,000 - $8000
Tables and chairs	$1500- $5000
Oven - no hood	$$750 - $3,000
Pannini grill - no hood	$800 - $1300
Sandwich prep cooler	$2500- $6,000
Stainless tables 6 foot	$200 - $400 each
Stainless (NSF) shelving	$ 300 each
Custom counters	$250 - $500 per foot
Designer or Architectural fees	
General contractor	
Tear out	
Carpentry	

Plumber	
Electrician	
Remodel interior	
Build bathrooms	
Finish floors, walls, lighting	
Signs and awnings	

Based on observations over the last couple of years, the following is a sample menu of the most common drinks with pricing included. Please keep in mind that these are only sample prices and that you should adjust your pricing based on your location, target market and your market sophistication.

Also note that we have not included food, snack, gifts or other like accoutrements. These are items that are unique to individual shops and communities and should be priced and budgeted according to your needs.

Appendix B

Example Menu

	Single Shot	Double Shot	
ESPRESSO	0.95	1.45	

ESPRESSO DRINKS	Small	Medium	Large
Americano	$1.25	$1.50	$1.85
Cappuccino	$1.55	$1.95	$2.50
Flavored Cappuccino	$1.95	$2.35	$2.85
Latte	$1.55	$1.95	$2.75
Flavored Latte	$1.95	$2.35	$2.95
Café Mocha	$1.95	$2.50	$3.00
Viennese	$1.95	$2.50	$2.60
Turtle Latte	$2.00	$2.50	$3.25
Hazelnut Mocha	$2.00	$2.50	$3.25
Café Breve	$1.95	$2.80	$3.25

OTHER DRINKS			
Brewed Coffee	$1.05	$1.50	$1.85
Hot Cocoa (add flavor .15)	$1.25	$1.35	$1.85
Hot Moo	$1.25	$1.55	$1.75
Hot Cider	$1.05	$1.50	$1.85
Hot Tea	$0.95	$1.25	$1.50

COLD DRINKS			
Italian Cream Soda	1.5	1.85	2.25
Italian Soda	1.35	1.55	1.85

Granita	1.55	2.15	2.85
Iced Tea/Cider	1.05	1.5	1.85

Extra Whipped Cream .20

Extra Shot of Espresso .75

Appendix C

Espresso Equipment Descriptions

ESPRESSO MACHINES

The Victoria Arduino two-group vertical model (pictured) is made by Italy's oldest commercial espresso machine manufacturer. This is a very traditional look, whether in single group, double or triple as well as compact are often chosen when an owner wishes, to "*make a statement*". Versions for homes are also available.

SUPER AUTOMATIC machines are available from numerous manufacturers and in model designs that range from almost $25,000 to as low as $5,000. The term SUPER AUTOMATIC usually refers to a machine that has one or two a built in grinders and a refrigerator. It can grind the beans, dose the correct amount, make espresso and froth milk into a cup, stop itself, discard spent grounds and cleanse itself after every drink; all with the press of a single button.

The standard or traditional espresso machine is usually manufactured to be either a semi-automatic or an automatic. Semi-automatic means it has one control button per group head. Press it once to start water flowing and press it again to manually stop the flow.

Automatic machines have a programmed panel of several buttons for each group. One press of a button causes the machine to deliver a pre-determined amount of water before automatically shutting itself off to stop the water flow. Traditional espresso machines of commercial quality range in price from around $13,000 down to as little as $3,000.

The pictured VIP is a full size two-group machine with numerous bells and whistles.

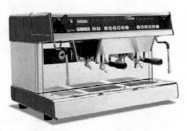

It has a timer to turn itself on and off, counts every drink, can be linked by a modem, has a self diagnosis trouble shooting system, built in security controls, can be programmed in several languages, tracks maintenance by drinks volume and time, has a raised group to Permit 20-ounce cups to be placed directly under the portafilter.

Most manufacturers also produce a full size model that offers similar volume capacity but is more affordable by removing some of the bells and whistles. The pictured model is such a model, with out the sophisticated electronics built in.

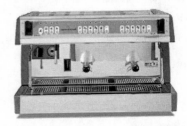

Many times counter space is an issue. Manufacturers build machines of a more compressed size to meet this need. Roughly 50% of the space and cost gives buyers about 90% the production of a full size machine. Most commercial single group machines are connected directly to a water line and use only 110v of power.

Certainly, a great number of machines sold in the world are single models. These compact commercial models are also often purchased for homes & offices.

A recent development in espresso is something we call a POD. This is pre-ground, pre-measured and packed coffee into two-sided paper. The pod is sealed inside a foil pouch for freshness. Almost all-traditional machines can be modified to make use of pods, and now some machines are designed specifically for use of pods.

SAMPLE GRINDERS

This GRINTA grinder is what we call a compact. It holds about ³/⁴ pound of coffee and is only about 6 inches wide. It grinds a pre-measured amount of espresso at the touch of the control plate. This is an ideal grinder for decaf beans or for smaller operations selling less than fifty drinks daily.

This MDX is a full size standard espresso grinder capable of holding up to 3 pounds of beans. It can grind coffee as fast as you can make drinks. The infinite grind feature helps maintain consistent drink quality and also makes it easy to open and clean without losing the previous grinder setting.

The MCD-65 is a bulk grocery style bean grinder in the European design. It has settings permitting the grind to match any brewing device and a spring handle to hold a bag while grinding for retail sale.

Photos courtesy of and © Nuova Simonelli™, Italy

Appendix D

Espresso Basics

Photo's Provided and © by Nuova Simonelli™

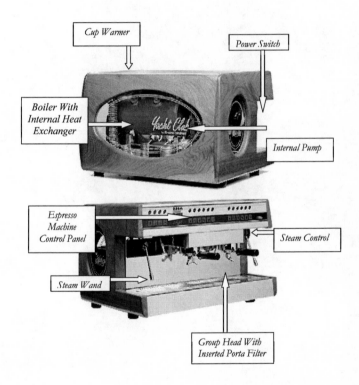

Cup Warmer

Power Switch

Boiler With
Internal Heat
Exchanger

Internal Pump

Espresso
Machine
Control Panel

Steam Control

Steam Wand

Group Head With
Inserted Porta Filter

Appendix E

Your Porta Filter and You

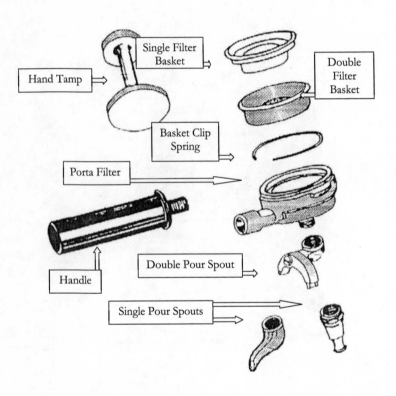

Hand Tamp

Single Filter Basket

Double Filter Basket

Basket Clip Spring

Porta Filter

Handle

Double Pour Spout

Single Pour Spouts

Appendix F

Brewer Essentials

Photos provided by NEWCO™ and FETCO™

The most important thing to consider before buying your coffee brewing equipment is how well that equipment will serve your needs the best.

One of the most common problems for all coffee shop owners is not having the ability to meet their volume demands in a timely fashion. The two models shown on this page use, what is commonly called, a "Gravity Pot". Gravity pots have the advantage over air pots in a number of different areas.

First, there are fewer moving parts on a gravity pot and that helps you to avoid both service and replacement costs.

Secondly, a gravity pot will let you brew and hold a higher volume of coffee allowing more time for espresso drink preparation.

There are also advantages to smaller, more compact air pots. Brewing in smaller batches helps cut down on waste and, at a lower volume location, helps to preserve the freshness of the product.

Index

Drugstore ZEN Press
Because Anonymity Sucks
www.drugstorezen.com